Sightlines

For Samantha,
Who knows the sorrow
 of life's fragility,
 and joy at its tenderness
that forms the sightlines for this
collection of poems.
 May all manner of things be well!
 JB
 Janet Grace Riehl

Sightlines
A Poet's Diary

Janet Grace Riehl

iUniverse, Inc.
New York Lincoln Shanghai

Sightlines
A Poet's Diary

Copyright © 2006 by Janet Grace Riehl

All rights reserved. No part of this book may be used or reproduced by any means, graphic, electronic, or mechanical, including photocopying, recording, taping or by any information storage retrieval system without the written permission of the publisher except in the case of brief quotations embodied in critical articles and reviews.

iUniverse books may be ordered through booksellers or by contacting:

iUniverse
2021 Pine Lake Road, Suite 100
Lincoln, NE 68512
www.iuniverse.com
1-800-Authors (1-800-288-4677)

The Lakeside title page photo—"Water Ceremonies" photographed by Crystal Daniels

ISBN-13: 978-0-595-37499-1 (pbk)
ISBN-13: 978-0-595-81892-1 (ebk)
ISBN-10: 0-595-37499-9 (pbk)
ISBN-10: 0-595-81892-7 (ebk)

Printed in the United States of America

For Julia and All

Be patient.
This is still the same story.
It will all come together in good time.

—Erwin Thompson, author's note
The Second Mile, Part 2

Thanks To...

Anna Riehl, my grandmother, and Erwin Arthur Thompson, my father, for the writing genes. The latter for permission to include his poems and draw from our family photo archive. Thanks, Pop, for sharing 90-years of family stories and guarding their historical accuracy.

Clive Matson, who said I could.

Hal Zina Bennett for navigating the sightlines of publishing my first book. He has the territory well-mapped, and kindly lent his compass.

Janean Baird, Nathan Aaron Bennett, Carol Cole-Lewis, Melissa Drew Stump, Kevin McCarthy, and Connie Pivoda—Graphics Angels.

Diane Thompson, for proofing.

My brother, an Eagle Scout at an early age, still earning those merit badges. I am the never-to-resign President of the Gary Arthur Thompson fan club.

All the family members and friends in Southwestern Illinois who form Team Thompson, caring for my parents and the homeplace.

Daniel Holland, my sweetheart, who shares his cozy home with me on the shores of Clear Lake.

Friends. A string of pearls that I found on the bottom of my jewelry box. The pearls were scattered, but some strong string fixed that.

Stephanie Ann Farrow, the many-faceted ruby at the center of my friendship necklace for three decades (and counting) on three continents.

The Rigpa Sangha and Sogyal Rinpoche, the string and clasp of the necklace.

Contents

PREFACE xv

SKEETER
BLOOD ON THE HIGHWAY 2
BLOOD ON THE HIGHWAY:
Two Lives and Two Deaths 3
JULIA 5
JUST LIKE YOU AND ME 7
AMELIA'S DOUBLE RAINBOW WISDOM 16
POULTICE 18
VALENTINE 20
REAPER 24
MAIL CALL 27
RED BALLOON 29

SLIM
POP'S PRAISE POEM 32
REHEARSAL FOR PAPA'S SONG 34
KING'S SAKE 36
GROOMING POP 37
HEARTBEAT 39
LETTERS 40
STRING BRIDLES 42
WRITERS 44

SCRIBBLER	45
STOMACH	48
THESE HANDS	49
LOVE UNDER YOUR NOSE	50
SWEEPING	51
TREASURE CHEST	52
YOU BETCHA!	54
DARE DEVIL	55
ECHO	56
NESTING	57
I DREAM OF JEANIE	59
COMPLAINT DEPARTMENT	60

SWEET LITTLE DOVE

PRAISING MOTHER	62
MAMA'S SUITCASE	65
UNDER MAMA'S YEW TREE	67
TOWHEE #1	68
QUEEN FOR A DAY	70
QUEEN BEE	71
WALKING MEDITATION	72
GRANDMA'S NEW LOOK	73
ROOM SERVICE	74
SAFETY PIN	75
LOTUS EATER	76
CATECHISM	77
CROCUS	79
SIGHT FOR SORE EYES	80
WORKING GIRL	81

SCROLL	82
BUTT WIPES	83
SHIT TO CAKE	85
STREAKER	86
ALARM	87
SCARE	90
APPETITE	92

HOMEPLACE

RISING	94
MUSE BRUISE	96
MORNING PRACTICE	97
POPE IN MY BEDROOM	99
WINDOW FRAME	101
KNICK-KNACKS	105
PAPER	106
CRAZY SEWING BOX, SORTING	107
BEES KNEES	109
MY GIRL'S LIFE IN MY PINK ROOM	113
DOLL WORLD	116
CALL OF THE RAILS	117
GRACE	121
AUNT GRACE'S HOUSE	123
BULLS-EYE	125
CHICKEN	126
GATED COMMUNITY	128
BUS RUN	131
HORSE HEAVEN	132
FIVE-HORSE HITCH	134

GULLY	135
LOVING LIBERTY	136
WHAT DO THEY KNOW?	137
MISSOURI AUCTION	139
UP UNDER THE PINE ROWS	140
WALKING RIEHL LANE	142

LAKESIDE

PHONE CALL	148
CLARIFYING QUESTIONS (AND ONE ANSWER)	149
SHUTTLE SERVICE	150
HOME SWEET HOME	151
QUAIL VISITATION	153
BODY BUDDY	154
FOURTH "R"	155
CIRCLING AROUND HOLES	156
ASHES WASHED CLEAN	157
FALL AT THE LAKE	159
STAY A LITTLE LONGER	161
ANNIVERSARY	163
About the Author	171

Preface

On August 16, 2004, my sister Julia Ann Thompson, 61, was killed in a car wreck. Julia's work as a world-class physicist, coupled with her far-reaching efforts for equality and justice, made a profound difference in the world.

Julia's husband, Dave Kraus, and my mother, Ruth Thompson, were severely injured in the accident. Julia and Dave's grandson, Cody, was pulled out of the car by a Good Samaritan. Dave, through skill, care, and willpower, slowly traveled from hospital bed to crutches to cane to walking unaided to driving a car. Mother, after escaping death by a hairsbreadth in the hospital, spent several months in a nursing home mending her broken arm and ankle. Cody appears to be back to a relatively normal boyhood.

In the year following my sister's death, I spent the bulk of my time in Southwestern Illinois at Evergreen Heights, the home pioneered in the 1860s by my Great Grandfather Riehl, and our homeplace still. I wanted to come closer to the family core, and be part of building a fire we could warm our hands around.

For my 56th birthday in December 2004 I went into a small retreat at King's House, run by the Oblate Fathers of Mary Immaculate in Belleville, Illinois. During this time, I came to a strong sense that the world is charged with meaning, and that *is* a poem. Not *could be*, but *is*. The only trick is to tease out the meaning.

In January 2005 the book began. Drinking morning tea out of an old-fashioned shaving mug, surrounded by enough antiques to make a collector drool, I cocked one ear towards my inner voices and the other for sounds of my parents stirring downstairs. When I heard them on the move, I dropped whatever I was doing to rush to help my mother get dressed and ready for the day.

The work moved back and forth between my Midwest home to my Northern California home on the shores of Clear Lake where the whirl of extended family, visitors, and renters of the Midwest quieted to just me, my sweetheart, and an old cat.

In childhood, I often watched my sister Julia put together 1,000 piece jigsaw puzzles. Putting together this poet's diary has been a little like that. It's a chronicle of my family and I picking up the puzzle pieces of our lives, studying them in light of Julia's absence, and then looking where to place the next piece. Sometimes we get just the right fit. But there are a pile of pieces still waiting to be sorted.

Mortality became keenly real to me over the past year as my parents and I aged together and we marked the anniversary of Julia's death. The sorrow of life's fragility, and joy at its tenderness, form the sightlines of this collection of poems.

Skeeter

She was the littlest human I'd seen all day long. A long way from the soldiers that fell into formation in front of me that morning. I called her Skeeter, my baby mosquito.

—Erwin Thompson,
recollecting Julia's nicknaming

BLOOD ON THE HIGHWAY
by Erwin A. Thompson

Blood all across the highway.
The death. The grief. The pain.
Two generations later
We see it all, again.

A life, still young,
And in her prime.
Cut short, and ended
years before her time.

There was a question raised, one time,
The hours that she had logged.
Always busy, on the run;
Looking out for the under dog.

Almost three-quarters of a century ago
My mother died in a similar way.
No warning 'ere that final call.
No time or need to pray.

They both scattered seeds of kindness and good will,
As o'er this world they roamed.
I know they both were ready
When God called them home.

BLOOD ON THE HIGHWAY:
*Two Lives and Two Deaths—
Anna Riehl & Julia Ann Thompson*

by Erwin A. Thompson
Son of Anna Riehl
Father of Julia Ann Thompson

My mother, Anna Riehl, whose heritage can be so clearly seen in Julia's life, was also killed in an automobile accident. She was struck in front of her home on October, 1929. She had just handed out-going letters to a bus driver who picked them up as a favor to take them to the post office. Such a practice is probably hard to understand in today's modern whirl. The letters were part of handling the family business of a small manufacturing company, Gladacres, on the outskirts of Rushville, Illinois.

The road in front of her home had just been paved two years before. Most residents and motorists still viewed it in about the same way as when it was dirt. Because the driver who hit my mother had such poor vision, she was not aware that she had hit a person. My mother was dragged several hundred feet after first body contact.

I was not quite fourteen at the time. I remember looking at the spot where she was struck down. The road ran red with her blood. I never saw so much blood, even at butchering time. My friend, Mildred Moore, who stood with me at the time remarked: "Death's blood will not wash off!" Undoubtedly it did wash or wear off of the pavement in the passage of time, but it has never washed out of my memory in the three-quarters of a century that has passed.

My mother's untimely death was a great loss to the family and to the world. She had been a helpmate to my father in his more than six years as the architect and construction supervisor for the Methodist Mission board in Korea between 1908-1914. In Songdo, he designed and supervised the building of one of the first girl's schools in Korea. The Korean peace treaty was signed in this same building.

In addition to supporting my father, my mother taught classes for Korean women and others for boys. She taught the women to understand the teachings of the Bible and its practical applications. She taught English and other worthwhile subjects to classes of boys. World War One put an end to my parents' missionary work, as the Board of Missions refused to send them back out. My mother continued her unwavering support of the mission work on a local level. Her devotion to her church work and the primary challenges of daily survival for her family were unequaled in my experience.

Julia reminded me of my mother in many ways. She had the same Spartan approach to life. Certainly, neither woman was one to show off her social position with fancy clothes. Julia forged lasting friendships with the Russian people she worked with in an international physics project mostly carried on in the Russian headquarters for science research in Siberia. Julia was instrumental in helping at least one Russian couple immigrate to the United States and become citizens.

Julia spent much of her own time and her own money initiating a program to encourage minority students get started in the field of physics. She found fulfillment in furthering projects most people would have considered impossible, or at least impractical. Surprisingly, in most cases, they worked!

With all of her involvement in scientific projects, Julia still found time and energy to devote to her family. She could be found taking her granddaughters out in our little rowboat or baking traditional German Christmas cookies. Julia, like my mother, will be missed not only by her family, but also by the world.

Julia Ann Thompson will be remembered for what she did and for who she was.

JULIA
by Erwin A. Thompson

She will be remembered
For what she did,
For who she was.

Her family gathered at Evergreen Heights,
The Home Place.
Not just blood relatives,
But her family
From all around the world.
Czechoslovakia, Russia.

From Maine to California
With Pennsylvania, Wisconsin, Illinois in between.

People she had touched;
Helped, inspired, guided.
Their hearts were heavy
With their loss.
Our hands touched.
We shared our tears.
Our memories of Julia.
Of what she did.
And who she was!

JUST LIKE YOU AND ME

Once upon a time a brilliant baby was born.
As brilliant as coal
under pressure for billions of years.
As brilliant as the diamonds
she never wore.
So brilliant, she dazzled us.

It was a virgin birth, you see.
Both parents were virgins when they wed.
They got busy changing that right away
because there was a war on.
Nine months later she came out,
all in a rush to get started.

She was just like you and me, only she wasn't.
She was a first-born child.
As if no other new life had ever
come into the world before.

Because she was the first,
all the firsts dazzled, became the stuff of myth:
First words.
First solid food.
First step.
First syllogism.
All duly documented and sent to Papa overseas.

She belonged to herself from the beginning.
"I'm not a baby anymore.
I can climb a tree.

Babies can't climb trees."
Thus, she declared her independence.

She practiced French horn sitting with legs flung
on either side of the birch branch.
The French horn anthem flung out
for the cows and horses to hear.
The branch tickled
the delicate spot where her own branches joined.

She might have taught little kids.
Mother did.
She dallied with majoring in English.
But, shoot! Why should she?
She can read and write poetry
in any language she wants without a degree.

There's this professor in a tiny Physics Department
at a Midwestern liberal arts college.
He hooks her.
Theoretical physics, of course.
No money for anything fancy.
He tutors her one-on-one.
At home, on vacation,
Pop turns her into a first-rate welder and mechanic.

Then, to Yale where they politely
cover their mouths when they laugh at her.
But, they're not laughing for long.
Not at all.
Now she's paired with a French graduate student.
Her Midwestern mind matched with his
makes for some interesting problem solving.

The smallest things attracted her.
She dazzled the physics world of subatomic particles.
Muons and *pions* knew no mercy
Colliding in the best accelerators around the world.
Cosmic Rays collected
in vats of water in a Utah mineshaft.

She's a woman in the right place at the right time.
She makes her own places and times.
When she gives birth to her daughter,
she bicycles to the hospital to give birth.
Her new baby sleeps at the lab
in the bottom drawer of her metal desk.

She was just like you and me, only—she wasn't.

She reads poetry in the original Russian
in Novisibirsk over cabbage soup
and a handful of carrots
thrown in from her backpack.
Demonstrates science experiments
in South African schools.

Pigtails flying.
Men's pleated pants.
Button-down shirts.
Round-toed tennis shoes.
So square she was cool.

She's just like you and me, only—she's not.
She doesn't seem to tire.
She's focused like a laser.
She wakes up with her priorities
typed on her forehead.

Ich bin ein Berliner!
Nosdarovia. Who sneezed?
Eto Baba!
Ich liebe dich.
Over there! A little to the left.
Ootsoheelay jang?
Keetsoheelay sintclay.
Njdigeazoora Ra.
I'm going to bed now, are you coming?

Then the light goes off for four hours sleep.
Hair comes down
to don a flannel nightgown
with little flower prints and ruffles.
(Can you believe it?)
That cute, sexy smile.

Next day, back to managing her empire.
Emails and phone calls around the world.
Students to mentor.
Women professors to counsel and escort
through the tricky waters
of sexual harassment and tenure.

Money to find. Grants to write.
Equipment to design, build, and fix.
Experiments to oversee and write-up.
Children and grandchildren.
Mother and father to care for.

Mohomaswe.
Horeelahoray.
I made 30 Apple pies last night.
Monatay taaaaaaata.

Entonces, damas y gentes,
encantada trabajar con tigo.
Your sunbonnet is in the bottom drawer.

If it's 3 a.m. in Illinois,
then it's x and y and z o'clock
in London, Russia, and Cape Town.

Julia studied physics, but her world
didn't conform to the physical universe.
"To her last second, Julia accomplished everything
possible and impossible in this life,"
as Vladimir Subbotin says.
She lived unbounded by time, space, and energy.
Julia's world moved to it's own equation
that only she knew how to solve.

She carried her duty, and more.
One favorite poem rehearsed her
for her death.
Boris Pasternak's "Hamlet"
from the novel *Doctor Zhivago:*

I...agree to play this heavy role.
But another drama now starts on.
...it is defined—the action's order,
And the road's end can not be sealed...
To cross life is not to cross a field.

CRASH.
The woman driving the SUV
had argued with her daughter.
Passed three cars.
Didn't have a chance to see the red light.

The superior force of her vehicle
creamed the driver's side of the little compact.
Blunt chest trauma
for our brilliant baby.
The ambulance ride
an expensive nod to a maybe.

A Good Samaritan
pulled her grandson out of the backseat.
The car burst into flames.
Firemen and policeme, matter-of-fact heroes.
"Just doing our jobs,"
they said when we thanked them later.
Her husband and mother airlifted
to a big-city hospital.

The woman and her daughter
crawled out of their SUV.
Nary a scratch.
Sat on the curb, stunned,
at what their car had done.

Good-bye, Julia.
Good-bye.
Good-bye.

A week later others went to see
your body at the morgue.
But, I stayed home
with your granddaughters.
Mother still hung by a thread in the hospital.
Would seeing your body
have made your death
more real and final to me?

Daddy didn't think it good for me.
He knows me so well;
I'm sure he was right.

Amelia and Maggie and I made art upstairs.
Amelia metamorphosed into Art Impresario
and displayed all our work downstairs,
scripted and choreographed.

(She showed me a special hiding place
where she kept a treasure map
only Grammy Julia knew about.
It became our secret.)

They came home with your watch
and gave it to Amelia.
"Off your refrigerated wrist,"
was all I could think of.
But, Amelia wore
the clunky watch as a devotee.
Even cinched at its last hole
it fell off her warm, skinny wrist.
She lost the watch. We all panicked.

But, the watch came back
to watch over her.
That $10 plastic watch knew
what time it was all over the world.
That watch meant the world to Amelia.
The World of Grammy Julia.

Your heart stopped, Julia,
but your watch ticked on.

Your myth ticked on.
Your spirit ticked on.

It had been hot.
Then started to rain.
A scout went to the side lawn and saw it.
A rainbow.
Not just one rainbow, but two.
One inside the other.
A stairway to heaven.
The scout came inside and called us.
Amelia and the rest of us bolted outside.
"Look, it's Grammy Julia going up to heaven!"

The colors, vivid. Appearing, yet insubstantial.
ROY G. BIV
Knock-your-retina-out red.
Off-shore orange.
Van Gogh's sunflower yellow.
Green, green fields forever.
Blue sky mind.
Indigo Bunting.
African violet.

Tibetan Buddhists say rainbows
are signs of realization.
Did all my sister's good works
take her over the top?
Julia, were you a secret yogini?
Amelia thought so.

She stood there, channeling rainbow wisdom.
"You see, when a good person dies,

they send a rainbow down
to fetch that person up to heaven."

I ran into the house afterwards
to write it all down.
Goodness, the girl was touched by an angel!
I sent her little rainbow-glazed teacups later
to mark this wisdom moment
just after her 8th birthday.
They're too nice to use.
We just look at them
on the top shelf of her china closet.

I can picture you as an angel, Julia.
Watching over us all, as Gary says.
You deserve the best you can get
what with all the good you did.

I can see you
up there in heaven directing traffic.
"Oops! Careful there.
That's one dangerous intersection, folks."

I bet she bakes pies
for the man up in the sky himself.
Darns the elbows of the choir robes.
Sends down solutions
for Physics equations in secret code.
Yup, girl.
You're my favorite angel.
And you know what?
You still dazzle me after all these years.

AMELIA'S DOUBLE RAINBOW WISDOM

Like a bridge up to Heaven, perhaps.
The sunset is like that, too.
Angels climb onto the sunset, trees, and skies.
These are the gates of Heaven.

A week after a good person dies
then a rainbow happens.
The rest rise up on a sunset.
The special angels like Grammy Julia
go to Heaven on a rainbow.
It's a bridge. An archway to Heaven.
The best people earn an Express Trip to Heaven.

The rainbow takes you quickly
and gloriously up to Heaven.
Especially if it's a double rainbow.

When I was small, when I was four,
Daddy said, "Stop the car! See?"
We looked smack together on a double rainbow.
You're more likely to see all the colors then.

It's a glorious sight to see a double rainbow.
Pouring full strength in the country.
Looking at the glory of it.
Heaven is a place where each angel
finds the place where they used to be.

It makes me sad,
but it helps in the long term.
The more I talk about her,

I'm crying less.
It might have seemed long to see the rainbow,
but only a few minutes had passed.

After the rain and talking up here,
everything seems cleaner, fresher, prettier.
From this height, especially, on this porch.
Did you know it is really a third story
if you count the basement?

We danced to the music of Rush for Gold.
I think Grammy Julia would have enjoyed it.

POULTICE
for Amelia Grace

She's looking for solace.
She's only eight.
It makes no sense.
It hurts to lose the one you love.
Any country song could tell you that.

Solace comes in a recipe for a poultice.
It's a wizard of a solution
Guaranteed to heal open wounds, sores, and so forth.
(Scrapes, scratches, and scabs).
Does losing your Grammy
come under open wounds, sores, or so forth?
Maybe all three.

Here's how to do it.
Take half a bulb of Star of Bethlehem,
two violet leaves
(either medium or big)
and a star petal.

It makes sense when you think of the wisemen
following that star of wonder, royal beauty, bright.
The violets shield her world
from ever being violated again.
Let's hope.

Mush up your Bethlehem Star bulb and petal.
Wrap a violet green around the bud mush.
Rub the fresh ointment into the open wound

until it's rubbed raw.
Place violet leaves over it to hold in the ointment.

Break the greens from wild onions.
Mix them up and eat right away.
Then you sing this song:
"Medicine of herbs and medicine of flowers.
Heal me strong and share your power."

Be patient.
Healing the wound
may take more than an hour.

Stairstep Threes (from right to left): Julia, Gary, and Janet

VALENTINE

Six months since Julia died.
Finally, writing thank you notes.
On Valentine's Day.
The day of love's fever.

We'd slept young years away, close-held bodies.
Legs wrapped the night.
Lay down, sister, and let me stroke your head.

It's Valentine's Day.
Finally, writing thank you notes.
Six months dead.

She came and went on airplanes and trains.
Spanned continents.
Subatomic explorations,
muons and *pions* accelerated.
Cosmic rays glowed in mine shafts.

Minorities and women in science.
Good works all around.

She came and went and so did I.
We criss-crossed the globe, but never flew together.
Three times she came on my home ground.

A high energy physics confab in Berkeley.
Then she slept at my place
on Crofton in Oakland,
after my second marriage broke its dam.
Washed and rinsed dishes, me drying.
I told her about Uncle Loris and Aunt Hilda's
muddy pond
where the boys held me down
until I had to limp home.

House arrest inside Grandma's house after that
in a witness protection program.
I scrubbed hundreds of African Violet names
off white plastic tags in her shallow porcelain sink,
thick slabs of homemade bacon, frying.
"I didn't know," my sister said. "I'm sorry."

In San Jose, another high energy physics symposium.
She shared her plush bed, a joke to her stark style.
Long talks at night.
Cheek kisses pushed the flesh against our teeth.
She darted in and out between meetings.
Wore men's slacks and button-down shirts,
her uniform.
Introduced me to her collaborators:
"My little sister."
Smiling. Our arms around each other's waists.

Mine with love handles,
hers stripped down.

Strangely, no pictures exist of just us two.
It's always in stairstep threes: Julia, Gary, and me.
Easter suits, hats and gloves.
Two Indians on the warpath scalping
their younger sister,
sweet-cheeked, in a pink-posied sunbonnet.
Leaning forward, bareback, on our pony.

The last time, she came just for me.
After I tripped and dropped my basket,
marbles flying everywhere.
She wound around curves and up steep slopes,
followed my directions like an arrow.
Slept at the bottom of our driveway,
wrapped in the night.
Mother's African gift quilt,
encircled her in the back seat.
But we were awake!
"I didn't want to bother you."

A whirlwind weekend.
Fast-paced, forced choices clad in gentleness.
Focused on results.
Perpetual motion.
Come out on the deck in the sun, Julia.
I learned sardine juice was good
drunk straight from the tin.
How precious to have her all to myself.
Clean studio but
crammed study at the end.

She spanned continents.
She came and she went.
Good works all around.
Now, for me,
time to hold my ground.

Six months since you left.
Cars, not atoms, colliding.
I'm writing thank you notes
on Valentine's Day.
This one's for you.

REAPER

How can life go on?
I didn't know why.
All day, I didn't know why.
Then, behind the computer,
the answer came.

Sunday, March 13th.
Our flower calendar
shouted her name.
One of the only birth dates
I know by heart.
Hers. Julia's.
Sometimes it's hard to say her name.
To sort it all out without coming apart.

Her 62nd birthday
and she's not here to enjoy it.
What a shame!

I didn't know how to say it.
Does saying it salt the wound,
or salve it?

At the end of the day,
late supper at the kitchen table.
It's her birthday, of course.
"Yes, a long row to hoe."
Pop's back hunched a little more.
His head hung a little lower.

Our hands locked in a vice grip.
"A special day when she was born."

In Little Rock, Arkansas.
Luckily he was out on pass from Army Camp.
Mother's water broke.
They barely reached the hospital in time.
No dilly-dallying.
No shilly-shallying.
She never was one for waiting around.

Is birth destiny?
That was Mother's theory.
Julia, like a rocket.
Gary's birth so perfectly normal.
Three trips to the hospital for me
on icy roads before I was willing
to come out and give it a go.

Her basic character set from the start.
She led the way.
Always had her say.
Strength shot through with a stubborn edge.
Both stood her in good stead.

On this birthday,
she lives beyond her death day
even though she was
part of the Reaper's Harvest.

The Grim Reaper is just about
the only one around who knows how
to wield a scythe anymore.
Yet, we all know how to sigh
once he wields it.

A full wagon filled with sighs
rumbles towards our weathered barn
behind the Big Brown House today.
If only there could be another harvest.

MAIL CALL

Has anyone picked up the mail today?
"Not that I know of."

It's a chance to get out of the house.
Not that the house is so bad.
There's no stink of death here.
Just the perfume of lives toward
the end of their days.
Just mortality hanging in the air.

My sister's death in a car crash
not so long ago
sends a message
from the master of skeletons
that we all know we are going to die.
We just don't know the details:
When, where, how.
Forget about "Why?"
Death just is, as birth is.
And most of us hope for an old age,
somewhere in there.

The daily mail run is a relief.
A ritual that passes the time
and marks our days.
It's a physical calendar
that requires physical action.
There's a result,
whether we like it, or not.

In these email times
mailed personal messages

have become as scarce as hen's teeth.
My sister's death upped the percentage.
Condolence letters flew in
from all over the world.
Six months afterwards,
that percentage has dwindled.
We are the only ones, it seems,
who still mark time with her life and death
as the dividing line.

Julia.
August 16, 2004, 12:25 pm.
Then, not Julia.

The raw rip of sudden death
stanched with time, is less jagged now.
Tears flow in different paths,
sometimes just wetting my eyes
instead of gushing down my cheeks
like a flooded stream.

At the bottom of our steep hill
I open the large red mailbox
at the end of the row.
Its paint worn and streaked over the years.
Filled today only with gimme letters and bills.

I tuck today's mail under my arm
and trudge back up the long hill
towards home.

RED BALLOON

We lost something treasured,
held by a thread.
We lost something unknowable,
a balloon shining red.

Red wore her well.
Burnished her light.
Light loved her,
but no halo in sight.

History holds her.
Been here and done that.
Death claimed her.
Sealed the goodness, and yet—

We lost something treasured.
A balloon shining red
floats high in the sky.
Wafts over our heads.

Slim

POP'S PRAISE POEM

Erwin Arthur Thompson.
Erwin Arthur Thompson.
Ur-win Are-thur Tom's Son.
Grandfather to David Arthur.
Father to Gary Arthur.
Son of James Arthur.

You collected nicknames in your life.
"Tom" they called you, and "Tiger" and "Slim".
A leader with never enough to lead:
Platoon, union, scout troupe, family.
The community that grew around
Mr. "Big Daddy" Thompson on Evergreen Heights.

Homespun Renaissance Man of culture and grace.
Clean plate for dessert after digging out water lines all morning.
Well-rehearsed folksy disguise over layers of armor and amour.
You open your inner doors a peek at a time, letting life
enter you like a cat tossed out in the rain.

You taught me to dance while I stood on your steel-toed shoes.
You taught me to sweep in your workshop.
In a family of teachers, you are the teachers' teacher.

Handy man and artist inside one package.
You like to fix things: cars, houses…people's lives.
Self-taught, self-made, you are American to the core.
Music, novels, poetry, carving are your frontiers.
Creating is…what keeps you sane.
Is your electrical conduit
between your intense inner world and us folks outside.

In service and in harness all your life.
Loyal as a trusted horse.
Your good deeds form your red carpet.
Your road to royalty.

You live on principle and purpose.
But, thank the Lord, Pop, you remember how to play.
"A little humor dear," you explain to mother.
The glint in your eye, your laughter, your stories
warm your craggy face and made our growing years fun.

REHEARSAL FOR PAPA'S SONG

"I couldn't say, exactly, but the song went like this."

Cold nights bind us together,
And in my silence his icicle words melt.
He tells of warm burrows in frozen time.

Fiddling and square dance calls.
"Ladies bow, and gents bow under,
Hug 'em up tight,
and swing 'em like thunder!
Grab your toe and on you go,
Chicken in the breadpan,
pickin' out the dough!"

Lulabelle and Skyland Scottie,
on the crystal set
"Country lads and lassies,
goin' to the scene.
Lookin' fresh as dewdrops
on a bunch of garden greens.
Gingerbread and candy
they're eatin' all the while,
Goin to the circus,
puttin' on the style!"

Jeanette Mc Donald and Nelson Eddy,
on the silver screen:
"He takes her in his arms. Would you?
Would you?
He tells her of her charms. Would you?
Would you?"

I learn slowly.
His time is mine only by heritage.
But when the revival comes,
his glacier music will need singing!

KING'S SAKE

The Old King is dying, and he knows it.
The Old Ways are dying, and he knows it.
The Old Music is dying, even as he plays it.
He tries to keep it all alive.
But no one is fooling anyone,
least of all him.

So much to do. So little time.
There's only one of him to go around.
Mom,
the place,
the new novel,
the old heritage for the archives.

You'll live at least to 99—another 10 years, yet.
"I might have said that three years ago,
but the last two have been mighty hard ones."
His body is falling apart, slowly.
Every time he gets a new ailment,
the doctor says, "Well, Mr. Thompson,
you will die with it, not of it."

The only thing he'll die of is old age.
Or, maybe old age and a broken
heart that keeps on breaking.

The Old King is dying.
Long live the King!

GROOMING POP

Coming home after a long absence, I say,
Pop, it's time we cleaned your glasses.
He yields them easily with a closed-lip smile.
Safety glasses stuck on my father's face for decades now.
Pits from bouncing pebbles,
splattered paint, grime. I washed his glasses
with hand soap and warm running water
in the bathroom.
Glasses back on his face, his grin widened.
"It ain't near as dark a day as you think it is."

We play music from his youth.
Intertwined melodies and new harmonies.
Taught these songs by ear, not by note.
His little lamb, I follow his lead.
Long stories in-between tunes, gracenotes.

In honor of an up-coming appearance
at the antique car and quilt show
I trimmed his winter's crop of hair.
Pop spread newspapers on the bathroom floor;
fetched the old metal stool.
Stripped to his boxer shorts,
he offered his shaggy white hair to my clippers.

His body is slumped a little more,
but still strong.
Handyman and steward to the land,
its buildings,

and down-and-out tenants
huddled in the bottoms where corn grew once.

A simple haircut with electric clippers.
The back of his neck
crisscrossed wrinkles, dirt-filled crevices.
I clipped hair off over his ears.
Pop, you need to scrub your ears when we finish.

I trimmed his bushy eyebrows while we were at it.
His beard?
"Now, I never let anyone trim it but me.
Definitely not those girls down at the barber school.
But, if you want to,
have a go and then I'll finish off with my razor."

He cocked his chin towards me.
Sweet milk to a kitty.
Be quiet for a few moments.
You don't want to be talking
when these clippers go over your throat.
Mouth closed.
Eyes soft.
A silent purr as I fussed over him.
Hair falls to the floor, a faint cymbal-brush.
Each clump and lock, as it falls,
a syllable of love.

His line will continue.

HEARTBEAT

Pixels of sly smiling pleasure.
Newest great grandchild lifted to a nearly deaf ear.
Yes, there's the heartbeat
that promises his line will continue
when his own heart rolls over and moves on.

LETTERS

Pop types at one of his three computers,
his back to Mom in a last-ditch effort
to harvest family history
from the leaf-crackling letters
that blanket his end of the long table.

On his end, letters dry and fragile
as fall leaves.
On her end, mostly cleared,
just enough to keep her happy.

His voluminous desk converts to dining table
for large family meals
filled with boarding house reaches.
There once was a boarding house here.
We have pass-through cupboards and
slide-through drawers to prove it.
The Girls did the work.
So Grandpa Riehl gave the Girls
Design Privileges.

A railroad spike moves over each line
of faded handwriting from a century ago and more.
It's his soul he's searching for.

His mother's letters from college.
Her sisters' letters to her.
His father's letters to everyone.
Uncle's letters from grade school written to father.
Aunt Nell's letters from Washington State.

His mother's letters from Korea.
His own letters to her.

He's got a system.
Not quite touch-typing, because he looks.
Definitely not standard
because he pecks without much hunting.
Wields four fingers, not eight.
It's his soul he's searching for.

It's an ever-growing family story
housed in the University of Illinois Archives.
How's your novel coming?
I'm ready for chapter 7.
"In a 100 years
who will care about my writing?
These letters will tell the tale."
It's his soul he's searching for.

String bridle on Mr. Henny, named after a favorite family friend.

STRING BRIDLES
by Erwin A. Thompson

Letter written at 13 to his mother, Anna Riehl, from Evergreen Heights to Glad Acres, May 2, 1929. Anna Riehl died the following October, the same day the stock market crashed, both crushing blows to the family.

I brought a little frozen bantie inside
to keep company with the one Aunt Em brought in.
They are thawing out.
One seems quite spry,
but the other is still half-frozen.
I just fed the other banties
a cup of cornmeal and some water.

Aunt Em didn't need the Bluff House this year,
so she let me play in it.
I have all my cowboys and horses in there.
We found the cutest little nest;
it belongs to two redbirds.
We felt the inside, after the Mama redbird flew off,
and it was empty.

Not long after our string bridles began to disappear.
Then, our line, and ropes, and halters.
The bird swiped all our string things to line her nest.

Now she has three eggs and is hatching them.
She can thank her lucky stars she is in there today,
for the wind was fierce this morning.
I took her some cracked corn to eat
if she wanted to get off her nest for it.

The banties look like they're recovering.
One isn't tip-top yet, but the other eats.
When I put him back in the basket,
he got out and perched on the register.
I put him back in and he got out again.
I have to hold him beside me with my left hand
to keep him out of mischief, and can't hold the paper.
He is perched on one part of me one second,
and on another part, another.

Guess I'd better make some new string things.
The old ones are tucked in her nest pretty well.

WRITERS

They keep two computers
humming at opposite ends of the room.

Daughter writes new poems.
Father prints out his old poems.

Daughter types vignettes for her novelette.
Father bangs out chapters for his newest novel.

Father keeps farm accounts.
Daughter checks his stock records,
requesting electronic delivery.

Father transcribes crackly letters.
Daughter struggles to keep up with his output.

Father sends emails.
Daughter sends emails.
Together they blanket the world with words.

Pipefitter, Union Steward, Scribbler

SCRIBBLER

His back warmed in front of the fire.
Stretched on the floor to read his words.
Words scribbled at work
as rain or snow fell outside.
A pipefitter couldn't work then.
Inclement weather days,
the company called them.
As union steward he negotiated contracts
with management whoop-de-dos
to get those days properly paid for.

Tucked in back of the locker room
while other linemen and pipefitters

gossiped and played cards,
he scribbled away in spidery handwriting.
School-lined paper in a blue cloth binder.

He didn't need a creative writing
MFA from a high-falutin' university.
He carried stories in his head.
They had to come out
or his head would burst.
He warmed his nest of stories
like a broody hen.

At night when he couldn't sleep,
clouds drifted over his muse moon,
salting plots and characters
to rain down on his lined pages.

Other kids prayed for snow days to skip school.
I won't say we didn't enjoy
snow cream, snowballs, and snowmen.
But we also greeted Pop at the door,
ready for the next installment.
Like Dickens' cliff-hangers
that first appeared in magazines,
Dad's stories came in serials.

Neither quite knew what might happen next.
Dickens and Dad wrote up to the cliff
and then left us hanging.

But, we got to write by proxy.
"What will happen next?"
"Will the boy get the girl
or will the girl get the boy?"

Dickens and Dad scribbled
sentiment and chaste romance.
In the gallery a huge cheering section
rooted for the underdog.

My father channeled Charles Dickens
without knowing it.
The haves and the have-nots.
A heart of gold beneath coal-stained clothes.
The joy of that first kiss.
(No need to say more.)
The happy ending, breath exhaled.

"An author only has one story,"
he advised over gingersnaps and ice-cream,
our late-night snack.
"Imagined in as many ways you can."

Pop wrote 40 books in intermissions of a life of toil.
A mechanical pencil
tucked in the bib of mud-caked overalls
marked cuts on boards
and scribbled words that still mark mine.

STOMACH

Back in California I give my Midwest cooking a rest.
Pizza out of the freezer passes for supper.

In Illinois I concoct elaborate stews and *spetzle*.
To cosset my father's appetite.
To help his stomach march through Julia's death.

His savor for life no longer sat
at the dining room table after the accident,
if that's what it was.
"We'll get through it,"
stubbornly flung over his stoic shoulder.
Her absence, his first-born, hard to stomach.
Punched us all in the stomach,
making it hard to breathe, let alone eat.

His pants lie low on his slim hips.
He sucks in the pain
like he sucks in his stomach.
"Slim," a work nickname from gasfitter fame
could still apply at 89.

His back bends over
as though to pick up an imaginary pebble.
By some slight of hand,
he's looked the same to me
since I had the sense to look.
I need to catch up,
to wake up to the march of his mortality.
How can I digest this news?
A world without him in it,
would be no world at all.

THESE HANDS

When I was a young tyke,
he tugged me along with a work-roughened hand.
His height shrunk as I shot up,
and then shrunk again as his body aged.
Now, when I put my hands in his,
they seem small for a man's.
Not the huge hands of the giant
from my childhood.

These hands play guitar, violin, and banjo.
Whittle small animals
from walnut trees these same hands felled.
These hands tended my knees
when I jumped out of a swing onto gravel.
My father's hands fix roofs,
and broken pipes.
They put in new septic tanks,
re-wire houses,
and grade roads.

His two index fingers
typed out a hundred thousand pages:
novels,
poems,
family history,
trip reports recording travels
to the far ends of the earth.

His high-school diploma laced with Latin
and the three days he went to college

for mother's master's degree when she was sick
served him nicely.

Heart and brain wire to these hands.
"Learning to serve."
That's the motto of these hands.

LOVE UNDER YOUR NOSE

When I smelled the love
under my nose,
my father's love smelled of:
pine pitch,
mud after rain,
and iodine on an open wound.
But, it was love all the same,
and would do nicely.

Adapted from "Yet Lost for Other Causes,"
Stories to Live By: Wisdom to Help You Make the Most of Every Day, 2005

SWEEPING

"Thanks for holding the dustpan.
I can't bend over right now."
My niece said this, not me.
I can bend over, just not hold broom, dustpan,
and sweep all at the same time.

It never crossed my mind that one person could.
Was I paired with my older sister to do this chore?
She swept while I held the dustpan at the ready?

Or, in my father's shop?
He taught me to sweep, after all.
"Flick, don't drag."
Brooms were tools learned to use well.
Small hands briskly flicked.
Short legs steady.
No strokes drug either forward or back.

No dirt swept under the rug.
A sweeping tale, I'm still trying to tell.

TREASURE CHEST

He labors in the grove of service.
Remembers flat tires, repaired.
Loans proffered for crises.
Then his somber face glows
with the light of a thousand-watt angel.

Memories of good turns returned
is a treasure he counts with care.
His treasure chest
of good deed stories is a full one.

Bureaucratic stupidity
circumvented to better humanity.
If there is a fetching young woman
in the story
charmed
with his wit, courtesy, and good sense,
why then, all the better.

War stories as WWII platoon sergeant
overflow a section of his treasure chest.
Sure, my father earned a Silver Star for heroism in battle.
A Purple Heart commemorates his war wounds.
But memories of gratitude
from men he trained mean most to him.

His eyes,
slightly filmy from cataracts, mist over
as he tells battlefield stories not shown in movies.
Lying in a base hospital bed,
recouperating from shrapnel wounds and gangrene,
Pop met a man he trained.

"Sergeant Thompson,
I'm alive today
because of the things you made me learn."

A buddy shivered next to my Dad in a foxhole.
"Tiger,
when I'm in a foxhole
with you,
I feel safe."
"You're crazy!"
But, Christ!
That's really saying something.
Shells whizzing over-head and grenades exploding.
How could anyone possibly feel safe?

Men in the barracks
brought in a local French girl to have some fun.
She needed money and food
for her family.
These GIs could provide both.
They passed her from bunk to bunk
until morning came.

Then these men were stricken
with amnesia
and sudden blindness.
She needed to get off the post fast.
My father, not part of the evening's fun,
escorted her to safety
as if ushering his dance partner
to the edge of the floor
when the music stops.

YOU BETCHA!

"Some people bet on horses.
But, I like to bet on people,"
Great Aunt Mim liked to say.

Pop still does.
He could go broke making good on his bets.
Some horses don't even finish the race.

"That's my $5,000 sweater.
There's a $1,000 plastic bin."
Gifts from tenants who skipped out
on their rent, as is their bent.

Leaving town with no forwarding address.
Where is the bookie
who'd make book on these bets?

He's not a gambling man,
but he plays for high stakes
and long odds in this helper roulette.

Sometimes his bets pay off Big Time
with lives turned around.
One thing for certain.
You can always count on Mr. Thompson
when the chips are down.

DARE DEVIL

He stretched full length
atop the weathered wooden sled
he rode as a boy.
My smaller frame
plopped on his back,
ready for a bronco ride.

Pop's steel-toed boots shoved off.
My stomach bucked.
The steering arm squeaked
around the snow-packed corner.
My dad expertly
dodged the snow banks.
Dark trees streaked by.

Finally, we drug our feet
and slid to a stop:
our short ride to paradise.

ECHO

Warm pool.
Daddy in the bleachers, watching.
I'm a salamander now.
I have a badge to prove it.
Not flying fish, not yet.
They do the butterfly stroke,
flying above the water.
Sound bounces off the tile walls.

Afterwards, a rare treat.
At the vending machine,
we share a Bit-O-Honey.

Nestled together in the Bluff House

NESTING

The door
to my parents' bedroom is ajar.
I poke my head
around the door and peek in.
There they are,
not a peep out of them.

Cuddled in Mother's hospital bed
he cradles her head under his armpit.
Pop grins his head off.
Mother looks like she died and went to heaven.
Not a bad way to go, when you think about it.

"Tuck your head under my wing
and go to sleep," Mama used to cluck
when I was her baby chick.

Here they are, nestled together,
under each other's wings.
Nesting, with no eggs to hatch.

I DREAM OF JEANIE

"Chop, Chop!" Pop says,
clapping his hands together.
"Aunt Grace wants cornmeal
and some of those home-hatched
eggs everyone brags about."

Your wish is my command, Master.

"You'll find the cornmeal
on the front seat of my car
parked down in the barnyard."

I scurry out into the cold,
wishing I had a genie
to command.

COMPLAINT DEPARTMENT

As I turn towards the kitchen,
Pop's voice stops me.
"We've got a complaint here."
You've always got a complaint, I say.
(Joking, I hope.)

"No, this complaint is from our charge.
Ruth Evelyn Johnston Thompson
doesn't like the feel
of the socks you put on her."

Okay, I'll contact the Complaint Department.
That would be me, it seems.

At Mother's bedside,
I kneel,
praying at the sock altar.

Sweet Little Dove

Way down in the valley where the lily first blows,
Where the breeze from the mountains ne'er ruffles the rose;
Lives fond Evalina, the sweet little dove,
The pride of the valley, the girl that I love.

Chorus
Dear Evalina, Sweet Evalina
My love for you will never never die.
Dear Evalina, Sweet Evalina,
My love for you will never never die.

PRAISING MOTHER

Born Ruth Evelyn Johnston (don't forget that "t").
Married Ruth Thompson, Erwin's wife and lover.
We called you Mother or Mama,
but not "Mom."
"Mom" is too much
like the women in the wax commercials.

You are an original.
Your own person.
A sociable eccentric.
Your will like a steel bolt through your character.
You fought and scraped and plotted
For what mattered.
You were never one to purr your way to favor,
rubbing against legs to be petted.
If you'd been born a few generations later,
who knows what history might have had in store for you?

Your grit the stuff of American legends,
I see you starting out
as a stock girl and ending up Corporate President.
Your feet so grounded they'd sprout roots.
Your head a computer, whirling out business deals.

Or, I see you sneaking into the army as a youngster,
Carrying the general's bath water,
And ending up five star general yourself.
Hair clipped close and held firmly under your helmet.
Shoulders only slightly stooped by golden epaulettes.

The general in you
incapable of small-scale projects.

You marshal resources and forces as you:
Make acres of quilts.
Cook roomfuls of banquets.
Plant fields of flowers and vegetables,
laying in stores for the winter.
Victory is yours, over and over,
as you pack
the productivity of two into one body.

Yet, for all your gumption,
your feelings, like old lace,
disintegrate in my hands.
Your magnolia petal soul bobs down the creek,
navigating shallows and peering into depths.
Delicate titmouse feather Mama, same as those
miniature birds you feed
before they dart into gourd palaces.

I write this wrapped in your masterpiece quilt,
appliqued with views of Africa
you crafted and cried over
for years during one of our civil wars.

One day I tore open a bulky brown package and there it was.
Exquisite, a sign of our peace, and mother love.
It's a woman's quilt.
African women stately and beautiful,
Pounding sorghum and cooking porridge over an open fire.
You were there when you were there.
The women loved you because you were you, of course,
But most of all, because you were a mother.
You were my mother.

Adventurer,
Observer,
Gardener,
Artist,
Seamstress,
Craftswoman,
Teacher,
Birder,
Square Dancer,
Financial Tycoon.
You filled your life with the challenge of yourself.

Now, I call you on the telephone,
a year after your stroke.
We nearly lost you.
You lost megabytes of memory.
But, you never lost yourself.
The more you forget,
the kinder and softer you become.
"I love you, Janet," you say.
And then, say again a few minutes later.
I love you, too, I say.
Then, the surprise word slips out:
Mommy.

MAMA'S SUITCASE

When I grew up and moved away,
Mama's talent for finding treasures
amplified to *transporting* treasures.

She showed up on my doorstep,
slipped inside,
and opened her suitcase.
The great unveiling.
Ribbon-cutting ceremony.
Art opening.
My Mama's suitcase, a magician's trunk.

She peeled back the brown tweed flap of her suitcase
as carefully as a bandage off a skinned knee.
Instead of the yelp of pain, a moment of startled pleasure.

Spring.
Still-damp iris newly dug from the ground.
On top of a pantry's worth of dishes:
>thick blue glasses,
>blue mugs with woodpecker handles,
>and tiny Delftware saucers.

Summer.
Square-dance dresses cushioned just-ripe tomatoes
that peeked up from gingham ruffles.

Fall.
A ready-to-put-in-the-oven
Thanksgiving dinner.
Complete with frozen goose.

Christmas.
A Christmas tree from our woods
with sap still on it.
A collection of heirloom ornaments.

Treasure left behind
left room for taking treasure back.
Dimpled rocks, cuttings from plants.
Old-fashioned quilts
from roadside stands,
regional recipe books.
Tourist pamphlets
with exact history of each place she visited.
Get those details right
for the trip reports to follow.
There will be a quiz.

UNDER MAMA'S YEW TREE

Carefully, carefully
she gathers the country to Illinois.
Maine ferns find new shadows
in Midwest loam.

Carefully,
only a trifle greedy,
she draws together, under her yew tree,
the country's foundations.

Rocks and rubble
from Gettysburg National Cemetery
and Long Island back yards.

In darkness the country
crumbles while yew-loam
shines.

First appeared in *Folio*, Winter 2001.

TOWHEE #1

It's a bird with many names,
according to its range.
Eastern Towhee,
California Towhee,
Spotted Towhee,
Rufous-sided Towhee.
Through canny hunting, mother saw them all.

Towhee #1, on her handicapped license plate,
her birdwatching merit badge.
A souvenir from a life long love affair with birds.
Swampy refuges to mountain meadows,
her spotting scope slung over one shoulder,
binoculars over the other.
Bird book in one hand and life-list in the other.

Later, more frail,
looking out the car window
for her flying friends.
"What do you see?
Is that crest orange or deep yellow?
Move the car an inch forward,
now two inches back.
Perfect.
Yes, it's orange."

Markers catalogued and another bird
added to her life-list.
She even keeps one for me,
the most reluctant of birders.

Why can't we smell the flowers and gossip
like other mothers and daughters?

Her search for rare birds spans the world.
"That's just a coot," disappointed.
There's a cinnamon teal sailing the water.
Nothing new here.

In Alaska's inside passage
she spots the Towhee.
Now she can die happy.
A life-list expires when you do.

QUEEN FOR A DAY

You have to have seen the show.
It aired a long time ago.
Three housewives
(back when we called women that)
lined up, breathless.

These Queenly figures
came from scrubbing floors,
not aerobics class.
The winner had the saddest story.

Then the announcement,
the crown,
the ermine trimmed robe, velvet.
Red, I suppose.
The promenade.
The applause.
Better than the Miss America paegant,
which came later.

Mom coughs.
I snap to.
Let me get you a glass of water.
"Oh, you shouldn't do that. I'll get my own."
(She thinks she can still walk.)
But, you are the Queen, I say, and mean it.
"Queen of what?"
This household. Your domain.

She rises from her upholstered throne.
Got your balance?
Stand tall, like the Queen you are.

If she's the Queen,
that makes me a princess.
But, in real time, I am a crone,
excavating for the tunnel
to become Queen of Myself.
This is it.

QUEEN BEE

Did you ever study
the life and love-making
of the honey-bee?

She mates in flight.
The Queen Bee flies high.
The strongest male
who meets her there
becomes the Papa Bee.

This is the way
we felt about our marriage.

—Adapted from 1998 letter sent by Erwin Thompson to the author.

WALKING MEDITATION

It's an outing that takes almost an hour.
Add 20 minutes to get to the starting gate.
Bathroom. Bundle her up
in a coat, hat, muffler, and gloves.
Pastel-striped gait belt over her purple coat.
Hands positioned on the walker.
Pointed in the right direction.
Open and close four doors.
Prop the last one open.
Lock the one behind it.
A short stroll to the ramp.
Each time she goes down a different way.
Today it's one hand on the grab bar
and one on the walker.
At the bottom, square up the walker,
move to the right
of the paving stones around the Buick.

And we're off!
Up the graveled slope.
Past the white cottage.
She rounds the Y where the forsythia and birch used to be.
Heads downhill.

At the bottom, we'll turn again.
Complete the loop at the top of the little hill.
That's the plan.

It's all painfully slow.
Pop walks beside her, hand tucked inside gait belt.
I take up the rear, wheelchair ever-ready.
A handy chariot to ferry her home,
just in case.

"We'll enter you in the 100 yard dash," says Dad.
I look down,
counting my steps as I track her heels.
Breathing in and out once more.

GRANDMA'S NEW LOOK
For Lori
by Erwin and Janet

It's a handy little beauty shop
that fits into a pocket.
As soon as we say, "Mom needs a cut,"
she puts her on the docket.

"Have scissors, will travel," she laughs,
and so she sets about her task.

She snips and cuts with gentle care
deciding just which way each lock should fall.
She wants to do it right, you see, or. . . not at all.

Twice a year Grandma looks
like a pin-up girl from sixty years before
when Grandpa scooped her off her feet
and carried her through the door.

It's Lori's smile and tender words
that makes the cut complete.
It's in those little things she does
that lets their spirits meet.

She's a beauty herself, of course,
and part of the family tree.
And twice a year she brings Grandma's beauty out
fit for high society.

ROOM SERVICE

I deliver Mom's pills, half banana, and full glass of milk
bedside.
We've never done it like this before,
but maybe she can take her pills while reclining.

The automatic lift button responds to my touch.
Whir, whir.
We're good to go.

I hand Mom the small pills, first,
the really important ones.
As long as she doesn't drop one or palm them,
we're in business.

She tosses them back and sips some milk
out of the cut crystal glass.
Here's two more.
Now two more.
Here's the last one—can you believe it?
Whew, she did it.

She takes a ladylike nibble from her banana,
and orders a bowl of oatmeal
from room service.

SAFETY PIN

Can you pin down safety?
Makers of safety pins think you can.
But they didn't count on my mother,
all comfy in her easy chair,
to reach and open the drawer
in the old Singer cabinet.

Childproofing a house is a breeze,
I'm thinking,
compared to motherproofing a house.

The thing is, in my eyes,
she's still the mother I once knew.
Not this new mother
I find picking her teeth
with the point of a safety pin
when I duck my head in from the kitchen

Angels, if you are there,
dancing on the point of that pin,
please protect my mother.
She really needs you.

LOTUS EATER

When Homer docked in the land of the Lotus-Eaters,
he knew exactly what to do.
Don't eat the flowers!

Lotus-Eaters lived in a land
time forgot.
In turn, they forgot all about time.
You could spend your life dreaming.
In this heaven of the gods
nothing nasty ever happened.

When someone dies there,
they drop down through the sky,
away from heaven.
The Lotus-Eaters wave goodbye
and in the next instant, eat another petal.
The dream floats on.

Does she know?
No.
Sometimes it seems as if she's about to.
But, she slides past it, soft focus.
We know for her.
She lives in a land time forgot.
She doesn't even know to wave.
She just eats another petal.

CATECHISM

Have you seen Mom and Dad?
No. Not recently.
How long has it been?
Quite awhile.
Where are they?
They aren't around anymore.
Why?
They died, Mom.
That's what people do.
I know that.
We all look forward to that.
I think that's a good thing.
Dad died?
Yes.
When?
Maybe forty years ago.
Why didn't I know about it?
Maybe you forgot.
That's possible. What else is possible?
I don't know, Mom.
Where are they now?
Up in heaven, I guess.
You've seen their graves in the Jerseyville cemetery.
Why didn't I know about it?
How many children were there?
Six.
How many of the family is left?
You, Grace, and Oscar.
Why didn't I know about it?
How many in my family?

Four, now, Mom.
You, Daddy, Gary, and me.
Who are you?
Janet, Mom, your youngest daughter.
You'll always be my baby.
Yes, Mom.

Every time I say, *Your youngest daughter,*
Everytime we count to four instead of five,
I hold my breath.
Will she plunk in the missing piece of this puzzle?
She's come close, a few times.
She knows Julia is there.
Somewhere, there's an oldest.
Somewhere there's a third child
she nursed from her breast.
But where?

Her heart would break if we told her.
Then, she'd forget in the next instant.
Only to break again, and again.
Every time she asks.
But, she never asks, outright.
She never says, "Where's Julia?"
"How's Julia?"
"I haven't seen Julia for awhile."
Then, I'd have to hand her the piece.
Then, she'd have to know about it.
If only for a skipped heartbeat.

CROCUS

I offer her the first crocus.
Purple in a red-orange vase.
"That was Mom's," she said.
Yes, Francoma.
Cousin Cynthia showed me how to spot it.
Highly collectible.
An amphora crested with spring.

She draws closer to inspect it.
Tips it up to drink the water.
She starts to nibble the leaves and blossoms.
Flowers, Mom. To look at.

But, what if essence of crocus
surging through her bloodstream
is exactly what she needs?

SIGHT FOR SORE EYES

It's a meltdown.
And, no wonder.
She just can't see.
The pulley that holds the birdfeeder
looks like a big bird to her.
Even big print is too small.

"I don't know what happened.
My sight.
It's been going down the last month."
That's precisely right.
The left eye was already gone.
Then, the right eye bled.
It happened overnight
and that was just about the end.

WORKING GIRL

Horseless,
Mother lurches from her chair.
Grasps the rolling chair-back.
Slaps the table edges as she tramples forward.
Gets to Dad's end of the table
and eyes his fragile piles, ready to paw them.
"Ruth! Leave that alone. These are mine."
"I just want to organize them."
"They are organized."
"So you just want me
to leave them alone and go sit down?"
"Yes. That's the way it has to be.
It's sad. But, that's how it is."

We eat at her end of the table.
Her things get cleared off twice a day.
Those she doesn't file underneath the tablecloth
or squirrel away in back of her shelves.
She has just enough cards,
books, and papers to stir around in.

Mother, do you want to go to bed?
"I can't right now. I have all this work to do."
Mother, you deserve a rest.
You've done enough work for one day.
"I have a big day at school tomorrow.
I have to get ready."

SCROLL

What are you doing?
Making something, Mom.
What are you making?
Look at the picture, Mom.
What's that?
A scroll, to write on.

Muslin, metallic rick-rack,
sparkly glue,
yellow paper the light shines through.
Honey locust twigs.
Heaped on the table.
A jumble that jangles her.

What's that?
Scroll-makings, Mom.
You taught me how to make things.

What's that?
Look at the picture, Mom.
It's a scroll, to write on.

BUTT WIPES

"Who's butt have you wiped today?"
My new slogan for getting through the day.
My own, sure.
Hurriedly, on the run.
Magpie, my five-year-old great niece.
Mom.
Butt wipes are beautiful

I have to go potty.
Okay, then. Let's go.
Little pot? Big pot?
I remember sitting on the little pot.
Dark wood with a shelf in front to lean on.
Many family butts sat there.
The Big People's Toilet, enamel and high.
Sometimes she needs a little boost.
Then, sits there, smiling, teetering on the edge.

Take Mom.
Are you going somewhere?
"Well, (all shy and coquettish)
I thought I might take a trip to the toy-let."
She lingers over the first syllable,
then hits the last one.
Let me get your horse.
Don't move a muscle,
or you'll set off your alarm clock.
There.

I walk backwards, in front.
We chat along the way.

She admires the passing scenery.
Moves forward in small steps.
"You are my guide."
Yes.

Light on, vent fan, through the door.
Pants down, ready for action.
Bottom lightly supported as she eases down.
"You inspire me."

I sit tub side. She swings her leg, waiting.
It's always the left one.
Cute, like a schoolgirl.
She wipes and wipes and wipes.
I meter out the toilet paper.
We flush and flush some more.

Let me give you a special wipe.
Oh, you don't want to get close to this mess!
I like to do it. It's my pleasure.
Aw, pooh.
You did it for me.
Her laugh breaks the tension.

She rises. I part her cheeks. She did a good job.
Pants up. Hands washed. Both of them.
Random smears wiped off the porcelain throne.
I *do* like it. It *is* my pleasure.
It's part of our time together.
Butt wipes are beautiful.

SHIT TO CAKE

The day starts with shit and ends in cake.
I'm shocked to see a glob of shit on my mother's back,
generally smeared around.
It's not her fault.
Daddy and I both stepped out.

The clean-up crew stepped in and scurried about.
Washed, dressed, fed and medicine down.
She's back on the road in no time.

Luckily, no one feels like shit.
Good news comes in.
A story of mine will be published soon
for a thousand dimes.

Grandma Anna's "On the Heights."
Great Uncle Franks' "Poems of the Piasa."
Papa Erwin's "Whittlin' Poet."
I'm joining them now.
Except their poems rhyme.

I'm so happy.
I bake a cake with pudding blended in to make it rich.
Shit yes!
But, today, we eat cake.

STREAKER

For my brother Gary Arthur Thompson

All afternoon he talks with her.
Cares for her.
Washes her hair; cuts her nails.
Tracks her
as if he's tied to the table leg
next to her chair.

One little minute, his eyes wander.
Her right hand unties her robe.
Fuzzy pink plaid falls away.
She leans forward.
Flips the footrest down.
With another lean she grips her aluminum horse.

"Gotta go! Mom's stripped."
He presses the red button.
This call ended.

On his way home, just past Beltrees,
he calls back.
"Got the Streaker."

As a naughty little boy
I'm sure he never thought decades later
he'd have to tackle mother,
naked as a new-hatched jaybird,
and slide her back into that fuzzy pink robe.

ALARM

Mom does a flopsie from her walker.
(Her horse, Daddy calls it.)
It dents the soft chair beneath her bottom.
Sometimes it happens like that.

Lightly,
I safety pin the string connected to her chair alarm.
But, not lightly enough.
"What's that?"
Your alarm clock.
(That's what Daddy calls it.)

Unpredictable as all get out,
she can dart out of her chair,
as fast as the titmice flit away
from the feeder outside her window.
Only she can't fly.

We have to ground her.
Going somewhere, Mom? Wait! Don't move a muscle.
I reach around her back to separate her from the alarm.
"What's that?"
Your alarm clock.
Daddy sometimes takes off the trip pin
to impress her with her own personal siren call.

Then, the litany.
Let me get your horse.
Okay. Push off.
Hands here.
Got your balance?
Stand tall like the queen you are.

That last always gets a chuckle,
but it works.

She points forward.
I walk backwards in front of her
as if directing busy traffic at the airport.

The well-worn path
between her chair to the bathroom
a familiar promenade by now.
Perhaps too familiar.
Is it okay to turn on the light?
I ask my father, resting.
"Sure."
Thump!
Roly-poly on her bottom to her back.
She's down for the count now.
I swear, really alarmed.

Daddy and Dave rush onto the scene.
Dave from the kitchen;
Daddy from the bedroom.
Get the hoist or try an arm lift?
They hoist her up under her arms and settle her
on the hard-back chair next to the computer.

She's shaken, alarmed at her sudden descent.
Daddy disappears.
Dave and I work to rebuild her confidence.
"I don't want to fall again."
You're okay, we've got you.
I strap on her gait belt.
(*Your pretty belt*, I tell her.)

The litany, once more.
Push off.
Hands here.
Got your balance?
She hesitates.
"Like this?
Is this what you want me to do?"
Yes, now stand tall
like the queen you are.
Here comes the chuckle.

We finish the promenade to the bathroom.
I guide her safely onto the toilet.
Thank God all her bones are in working order.
Thank God, this time,
it was only a false alarm.

SCARE

"Janet, come here."
Yes, Pop? I'm here, Pop,
I yell from the laundry room.
He can hear a buzz,
but doesn't know where from.
It's no good.

I drop the laundry.
Hotfoot it into the dining room.
She won't stir.
Her blood pressure
dropped 20 points in five minutes.

"We have a situation here," he tells me.
"Wake up, Ruth. Get ready for dinner."
 Nothing.
Hungry Mom?
Nothing.
"Ruth, you're scaring me. Wake up!"
Nothing.
Another stroke?
Ischemic attack before a massive stroke?

We call Virginia:
family friend,
nurse,
all around good egg.

'There's nothing anyone can do until she comes."
Eat then, so you can go the hospital if you need to.

Pop pecks at his food.
I fold laundry.

Virginia arrives from the other hill.
Mother raises her head to nod to her guest.
Blood pressure, again. Pulse quantified.
Conference.
Mother rouses.

Virginia, in the entryway:
"Not for your sake, but when
whatever happens, happens,
I hope you'll be here."
Yup. That's where I aim to be.
For my sake, too.

APPETITE

At the end of her life, so much left undone.
So much promise left to be won.
So much sugar left unspun.

So many recipes left in the book.
So many foods left to be cooked.
So many meals left to be tasted.
So many roasts left to be basted.

So many tastes left to devour.
Her appetite still grows by the hour.
Even her stomach growl shows power.

Collected in boxes, bags, and barrels
her recipes keep her up all night.
She comes to bed now, and we turn off the light.

Homeplace

RISING

Eighty-nine, both my parents are now.
Just yesterday
my mother caught up to my father at last.
As if anyone ever catches up to another,
especially, if that other
never ran away in the first place.
They are a tag team, my mother and father.
Running and catching, tagging and running.
And so it will be, I think,
all the way to heaven and beyond.

"You have the genes," a friend tells me
on my mother's birthday.
"So you'd better take care of yourself."
Yes, the Good Lord willing and the creek don't rise,
there are many years
rising up before me.

It's been over a month now
since I imagined the life of the world
without me in it.

Would the world love me
any better or worse?
Would it weep at my funeral?
Or dance?
If I waded out into the water
with stones in my pocket
would I become the lady of the lake?

Would the world remake me
into a saint or a demon

or just a human
grown tired of herself?

But, it's been over a month now.
The rain falls outside, not inside.
The creeks rise, swollen with the rain,
but the Good Lord seems willing
and moves inside my will
until everything creaks, swells,
and rises inside me.

It's been over a month now.
My parents stir
in their bedroom below mine,
in the oldest house in the world.

My mother snuggles
inside the crook of my father's arm.
Their bodies, stirring,
warming each other, still.

The rain falls outside, not inside.
A new day is dawning.
And I am in it.
As my feet hit the floor,
my old age rises to meet me.

MUSE BRUISE

I woke up, clumsy with early morning haze
and brushed the Poetry Box
with my pajama sleeve.
It hit the floor.
More precisely, its point
punctured the skin of my foot.
That woke me up!

The box full of magnetic words.
The kind of words designed
to snap onto a refrigerator door.
The words snapped out to grab me.
The words magnetized me.
Woke me up.
Then they settled back
down into the birch box.

It's oblong,
that box with cunningly made
mortise and tenens joints.
4 inches wide by 2 inches deep by 12 inches long.
On the hinged top
the craftsman placed a metal rectangle
with the heart cut out
so I can see the birth beneath.

When all the words tip out
surrounding my foot,
I see the solid heart
cut from the rectangle.
Serenely placed
on the bottom of the box.

MORNING PRACTICE

My slitted eyes conquer sleep,
and I struggle towards wakefulness.

I flex my knee.
It hurts.
My throat hurts.
Gargling with hydrogen peroxide
kills cells, but so what?

Downstairs the teakettle
takes eons to heat up.
Crank up the heat under the kettle.
Crank up the heat in the house.
Put out the trash.
Take the boiling water off the burner.
Pour it, steaming, into the teapot.
Take a gulp of the green tea.
and scald my tongue.

Start cooking oatmeal.
Stray into the other room to send emails.
Burn the oatmeal
through lack of constant stirring.
Rescue the oatmeal.
Spoon out the burnt bits
and toss them into the compost.
Eat the revised version.

Toss back the rest of my tea.
Gone.

Come back to bed,
completely jangled.

Is it too late
to chop wood/carry water
to brew another kind of tea?

POPE IN MY BEDROOM

There is a Pope in my bedroom.
Sitting in the chair at the foot of my bed,
reading and writing.
Mouth open as if to speak.
What's he trying to say?

Shall I go forth to do great things today?
No.
If I'm lucky
I'll learn humbleness and patience
kneeling at my mother's feet,
on her birthday.
Her last lessons to me.

I clean her shit off the floor.
Off the toilet.
Off her nightie and sheets.
Off her.
It's all over everything.
All over her legs down to her ankles.
All over her back and arms.
She stands at the sink
to wash her private parts
as I kneel behind her
to wash her nether parts.
I'm going to powder your bottom, Mother.
She, laughing,
"That's what I did for you as a baby."
I know, Mom.
That's why I'm doing it now.

Feet washed,
socks and shoes on,
before the long walk to her chair.
She sits at her command post
in the Queen's Chair.
She gazes as the red-headed woodpecker
attacks the house once again.

Everyday he tries to peck the house down.
So far, it hasn't yielded to his demands.
But, he has made quite a dent
in the trim on the corner
above the birdfeeder
where the other birds perch,
content to peck seeds.
But, then, he is a wood pecker, isn't he?

Upstairs in my bedroom
The Pope chuckles.
Secretly watching and listening.
Mom gives me lessons
while I give her care.
The Pope nods and goes wherever
Popes go.
Point taken.
Gifts received.

Racing towards the river...the Mississippi.

WINDOW FRAME

My chest is a window seat.
I hadn't got that yet.
Wow, this is nice.
I keep discovering, uncovering,
possibilities in my room.

It's light outside at 7 a.m. now.
Technically, we're still traveling
towards spring
as days lengthen and nights shorten.

But, outside, snow cloaks the Magnolia branches
wriggling in the foreground
against the bluffs, beyond.

I have a little room there, too.
But that's another story:
Of a coop,

placed on the edge of the bluffline,
with just the right heat
to raise spring chickens.

In my cozy room,
at the front of the upstairs,
I never saw icicles so clearly
as I do now.
Rippling daggers hanging from the eaves.
Coming from the sky and headed down
to moisten the spring to come.

It's the water, you know.
My father explained it to me.
As snow melts off the roof,
it drips down, then freezes.
When the icicles melt,
water bumps along the surface of the ice,
carving a new cycle.
These sickles slash through the air,
reaping water, not wheat.
Not yet, anyway.

It's all right.
Here comes the sun,
a blinding ball cresting the cliff.
A dark line suddenly
racing towards the river.
The Mississip, iced over in places,
boasts barges that plow the ice aside.

The cardinals are busy at bird feeders
dangling from the Magnolia.
Clear 70-degree days fooled her into budding.

These bird feeders, rigged with pulleys,
come in two shapes.
One a long cylinder and
the other an urn:
like a gift from the Magi.

No gold, frankincense or myrrh here, though.
Just enough seed to coax
birds to fly outside Mom's window.
Both feeders sway under plastic
domes…to slide off snow, rain, and squirrels.

The bird show is Mother's main entertainment
while she reclines on her plush throne.

Something that delights her.
The show playing outside the window
links her to a past she no longer remembers.

Technically, that is.
Her mouth
can't form the words
to tell of bird trips around the world,
spotting scope slung over her shoulder
and binoculars superglued to her hands.

But, she knows.
I can see it.
"The birds," she murmurs,
and her face lights up.

The sun, higher in the sky now,
still a blinding ball in the heavens.
But yellow, not orange.
There's not much display this morning
as it rises above the fog.

Of course we know the sun
isn't really rising.
This phrase is a remnant
from when we thought the world was flat.
And if we sailed too far,
we'd drop off the edge of the world.

KNICK-KNACKS

"Knick-knack, paddy-wack give-a-dog-a-bone.
This old man came rolling home."

The house is filled with them.
Knick-Knacks.
They are driving me crazy.
Why didn't Mom know that the more stuff
crammed into the room, the less you see?

Wherever they roamed, they collected them.
As soon as she came home, she hung them,
stacked them, and packed them.

The house is decorated in late Victorian revival.
All over the house, I find them.
Covered in dust and mold.
Eaten by mice and moths and weavils.
My favorite things ruined.

This morning, I've had enough!
I declare this a Knick-Knack Free Zone.

PAPER

What is it about you, paper?
You've really gotta hold on me.

Pictures, pretty, or meaningful.
Pictures, to send to others.
Cards. Things that could become cards.
Just pictures and little booklets
and things I like, or, could like.

Newspaper clippings on topics of interest
to me, to friends, and family.

Mother did this.
Sent envelopes stuffed with well-chosen clippings.
A message all on their own.
When I traveled alone across Africa,
Clippings warned me of danger ahead:
revolutions, rapes, and white slavery.
She didn't need to say a word.
The clippings spoke for her.

Now, it's "Have scissors, will travel."
Though, they have to be checked-through.
Even my plastic scissors raised the panic bar.
They weren't impressed that I was a collage artist.

Blues and jazz clippings,
Africa,
Poetry,
Quirky community Art.
Literary Reviews.

Paper, how do I categorize you?
Let me count the ways.

CRAZY SEWING BOX, SORTING

As if the sewing box were your mind,
jumbled yet ordered units.
As if brain cells wanted to retain
a memory—then transposed it.

Depression-era string-saver,
you rescued tail ends of thread.
Bunches wrapped tight in tiny packets.

Other thread all in a tangle,
a mass of undisciplined neurons,
transmitting random images.

You collected dainty boxes,
threw categories to the wind,
watched grommets, needles, paperclips
rub together.

Fasteners must have fascinated you.
Hooks and eyes, buttons, snaps, and zippers
pressed into service to mend scattered synapses.
A clamp for an absent nametag
searched for the identity of the lost wearer.

The last phone list ever used
on crumbling soft paper
in the same gangly hand as your son's,
only jerky. Numbers for police, doctor, children.
Help only a call away.

Among crazy daisies you spun
I found your wedding ring
snuggled next to your obituary
from the Sunday paper.

First appeared in *International Poetry Review*, Spring, 2001, vol. XXVII, no. 1

There are no chestnuts anymore.

BEES KNEES

Birds have knees,
to bend feathers
supported by hollow bones.
There are bees' knees, too.
Or, so they say.
I'd need a magnifying glass
to see fine golden hair on these knees.
An x-ray to see their inner workings.
Where there are no bones, how do knees bend?

Knees-as-symbol.
There are whole worlds of theories.
Flexibility. Support.
Cushions for those jarring bumps one encounters.

Yesterday, a mutt bit the back of my left knee.
I scratched his ears, and we grinned at each other.
I walked off, arm in arm with my chum.
Out of nowhere the dog rushed up and bit me.
Ouch!
Is there a symbolic meaning here
that's my duty to sort out?
Or, did a moody dog just bite me?

My friend salved it with grape seed oil and calendula.
When I saw the dog's owner, I said,
Your dog bit me this morning.
"Really? Did it break the skin?
Usually, that's all it amounts to."

I told my sweetheart about the bite.
"Which leg was it?
Your trick knee or your good one?"
The good one. Wanna see?
A clot of blood dotted the fang mark dimpling torn skin.
I'm lucky I had tough pants on.
Not rabid. Current tetanus shot.
But still. The indignity of stealth attack.
My good knee, now not good,
the now-bitten and assaulted knee gone bad,
will protest and heal.

But my trick knee
is still playing tricks on me.
In the bathtub I notice the angle
of my right knee doesn't match the left one.
It won't lie flat.
It wants to bend slightly upward.
"How did you hurt it?" my doctor asks.

Fierce cleaning.
I twisted around from the front seat of a car
to scrub out dirt and orange paint.
"Oh."
*I wrenched it again scrubbing the floor
behind the washing machine.*
My patella didn't like it and crunched.
*I hurt it again scrubbing tar spots
oozing across the pink vinyl floor.*

"Is that all?"
*No. I injured it again
when I got rid of the of barbwire
which cut the sightline down at my little Bluff House.*
A foundation and a back wall, really.
I sat in an old lawn chair to relax,
but made the mistake of looking left.
Barbwire stretched up and down the hill.
Don't fence *me* in.
I grabbed wire cutters, crow bar, and hammer
from Pop's workbench and went at it.
Dodged tree trunks and dove through brush.
Cut out the wire by sections
and drug it up to the winter garden.
Up to the lawn where the river seems so near.

At dinnertime I confessed I'd injured my knee
and lost the wire cutters—an ancient affair,
old-fashioned strength forged into the iron.
"You'd better find those wire cutters. I depend on them."
I retraced my rampage, scrambling with my cane.
Uphill, downhill. Where could they be?
He'll have my hide if they disappear.

At the base of the oak tree
where wire grew inside its bark hide,
the clippers lay at home base, my fears baseless.
I clipped both sides of the wire and had to leave the barbs in.
Galloping and galumphing.
That's how I twisted my knee.

"Is that all?"
Yes, that's all. Well, almost.
I pulled the barbed wire to the trashcans
where it curled into tangles.
Not knowing what to do next.

"That's no way to leave it!
The garbage man can't handle them that way."
We lassoed the barbs into loops.
Stuck them inside the bashed metal can.
The trash man rumbled up yesterday, and now the barbs are gone.

"What was fenced in or out?"
Cows.
They didn't want them to get into the chestnuts or fall off the bluff.

There are no chestnuts anymore.
But, there's still a bluff to fall off of.
A bum knee to bumble on.

How would I see all this as a bumblebee?
Knees streaked with pollen as I
dove to suck nectar through the stamen straw?

Wings fluttering fast against the wind?
Making a beeline to the honey comb
to sweeten another wax cell?

MY GIRL'S LIFE IN MY PINK ROOM

We'd fixed up the White Cottage really nice.
When I came down with the mumps,
Daddy stayed home,
read to me and put in an indoor bathroom.

Our family moved a few paces down
to the Big Brown House
from the White Cottage
when the Great-Aunties died.

When we first moved in,
he and I sat in the cistern basement.
Daddy, isn't it disgusting
that we have to start all over again?
Slowly each of the fourteen rooms,
five porches, and eight rooms in the basement
bent to fit our family of five.

Among Big Brown House mysteries
a $100 bill in the safe
in Gary's Cowboy Room closet.
Play money? No. Real enough.
We turned it in…for his college education.

The 1950s.
How do you spell "modernity"?
V-I-N-Y-L.
Vinyl floors.
With his seven-year-old apprentice,
we set about transforming the Big Brown House.
By the time we came to the room

that would be mine,
I knew how to do it by heart.

Nail down a plywood sub floor.
Strip the joints where the plywood comes together.
Spread black goop.
Roll-out tarpaper with its silver ghost markings.
Nail it down.
Watch though! That black goop easily sticks to skin and under nails.
It only comes off with an oily spirit.

We set up lines of string,
using plumb line.
Anchored string with small nails
to make straight rows.
Then spread tan goop
with a serrated-toothed trowel.
Finally, the pink-and-grey colored tiles,
laid in our own pattern.

We began in one corner and worked outward.
Checked the get-away path.
Tamped-down the finished floor
with a heavy metal roller, my favorite part.
The roller creaked and little bubbles pressed out.

Modern floors supported mother's refinished antiques.
I was crazy about pink then, as little girls are.
Pop didn't care much for pink.
Okay, he *hated* pink.
But, he did care for me, so pink it was.
Even wallpaper bloomed little pink flowers.

I slept underneath a double wedding-ring quilt,
part of my trousseau.

The carved walnut headboard loomed above my head.
Marble-topped dressers and, in the middle,
a round table of the sort
heroines in the old-fashioned books
I read might have taken tea.
Against one wall, a white china pitcher
and washbasin on a dresser
with a false top and secret drawer.

In my weekly ritual of changing the table-top tableaus,
I took ribbons from funeral biers from the potting shed
and twisted these into little nests
filled with wee baskets and figurines
I scoured the house for.

Treasure abounded:
Scraps of lace.
A wasp's nest.
Birds eggs.
Butterfly wings.
Tiny vases filled with lilies of the valley.

Altars I tended as devoted handmaiden.
Arranging tiny worlds I controlled.
Door closed as I worked,
brow furrowed in fierce concentration.
Hummed hymns of my girl's life in a pink room.

DOLL WORLD

"Elizabeth"—the name of queens.
An antique wicker baby buggy
her royal carriage.

Precious, my own.
I ruled this world by making the rules.
My doll followed them.
Or not, at her peril.
No crying, for instance.

But I bashed her head against the locked door.
My rage meeting his.
True, she had no brains inside her brain box,
but she cried none-the-less.

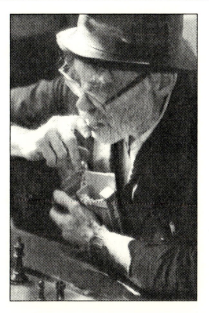

Uncle Willard let Julia win.

CALL OF THE RAILS

The TB thing is like this.
When I was five, my hobo uncle came to visit
just when everyone in the family
came down with mumps.
Because he'd already had mumps,
and the only adult in the house still standing,
he entered into a short-lived career
he'd probably never dreamed of:
nursing.

He plied us with beef stew and cherry tapioca
made with cherry juice instead of milk.
Its texture closer to a gelatin dessert than pudding.

He taught Julia to play chess—and let her win,
I bet, even though she's pretty smart.
I never got that far and,
being the youngest, stuck with checkers.

Not only had he had the mumps, he'd had TB.
That meant I'd been exposed and for the rest of my life
TB skin tests always came out positive,
making them a bum indicator.
So I had to have chest x-rays.

After Uncle Willard left us, he set up a bookstore
in his room in Portland. When I was ten,
we began our correspondence.
He sent me packages
of yellowed grade B Westerns.
These covered the sort of subjects
not quite appropriate for a young lady.
But, I loved getting these packages,
wrapped in brown paper bags
addressed in his sprawling handwriting.

In between the packages,
fat letters arrived with messages
spilling over the backs of envelopes.
It took me well into my 20s to break myself
of this habit copied from Willard.

His handwriting
might as well have been hieroglyphics.

I could make out only every few words.
Pop alone knew how to crack his brother's code.
He read these letters out loud at the kitchen table.
These letters told me about a gentle,
witty man who was my Uncle Willard.
Pop said Willard's intelligence
hadn't found its proper home.
The Great Depression, you know.
Instead of going on to college,
Willard took his education to the rails
and learned in the School of Hard Knocks.

I never saw my uncle again
after he nursed us back from the mumps.
My brother Gary went to visit him once.
Books piled from floor to ceiling.
Piles tumbled into every space
otherwise vacant. Gary was happy to leave
the acrid-smelling room, and take Willard out
for some fresh air and coffee.

When Willard died,
it took awhile before the authorities
found his body in the one-room bookstore
that doubled as his home.
The return address of one of my letters,
written so many years ago,
the only clue of next-of-kin.

I still have Willard's photo he sent me once.
A large black and white, like a PR photo.
From its glossy surface his gaunt, stubbled cheeks
sink below eyes framed behind heavy glasses.
His eyes look out from the picture into mine.

My cheeks are round, getting slightly grooved,
and rise to meet my reading glasses.

I don't read grade B Westerns anymore,
but yes, books vie for living space in my own room.
I've never tasted anything quite as good
as Willard's cherry tapioca.
And, if I listen closely, I, too,
hear the call of the rails.

GRACE
for four generations of Graces

Amazing, isn't it, grace?
        Praising.
        Blessing.
        Raising.
Hearts lifted in thanks.
How sweet the sound.

The Greeks named three Graces.
        Joy.
        Charm.
        Beauty.
Grace, a Lost and Found Department.
        Finding our ground
        Within the surround sound.

Grace cares—
        Cares for.
        Cares about.
Searches out the heart of the other.

Grace dignifies—
        The smallest loaf.
        The least fishes.
        The blinding flash of a moment.

Grace extends—
        Myself to ourselves.
        A due date that crept up
        without notice.

Grace clothes—
> In beauty.
> In kindness.

Grace attracts—
> Good fortune.
> Good will.
> Good music.
> Good merit.

Grace moves—
> In comfort.
> In elegance.
> In gladness.

Grace—
> Glides.
> Yields.
> Takes in.
> Embraces.

Grace—
> Lifts the veil.
> Finds our hiding places.

With Grace—
> We were blind,
> but now we see.

AUNT GRACE'S HOUSE

Aunt Grace's house greeted me with pies
ready to pop into homemade carriers
destined for diners and coffee shops.
Those lucky devils.

Cooling fruit cobblers
beckoned from her kitchen table
after kindergarten.
She set a slice on my plate,
blackberries oozing out from the tender cake.
What a welcome treat from childhood weight watching.

Aunt Grace's place was a playground haven.
A rope swing soared from the white pine tree.
Uncle Bill's homemade jungle gym
so homemade, in fact, that I once got splinters
in my butt when I slid down the slide.

Aunt Grace's hugs.
Held close to her curves.
Stopped the world outside her arms.

Aunt Grace's sewing machine
whipped up green saddle bags
with our initials outlined in tooled leather.
Who cared if they were vinyl?

She loved to tell the story
of how I crawled up to the brown cottage
to pat powder on Cousin Court's bottom.
How great to have a living baby doll.
Myself forever the family baby after mother

miscarried when she slipped and fell
down the basement steps
on her way to do the laundry.

Aunt Grace's house five decades later.
Attic mold.
Walls stripped back to lath.
Plaster peeling.
An Italian villa in Godfrey, Illinois.
She waits and watches; wants it to fall down
just before she dies.
That would save buyers the trouble of wrecking it.

She follows the news.
Grows herbs.
Bundles up in her 50-degree house.

She pulls out a chair from her kitchen table
to serve tea and cobbler.
But stops, first,
to give me a world-stopping hug.

Uncle Frank (right) hit targets around the world.

BULLS-EYE

Straight-shooter hit targets
around the world.
He pulled the trigger and hit
the bullseye every time.

He set his sights straight,
aimed for—and won—the title:
"World Champion Marksman."
No one in America or Europe
shot straighter or truer.
His favored ammunition said it
plain as day on the box:
the ammunition of champions.

Author note: *My Great Uncle Frank, besides being a World Champion marksman, played violin and wrote three books of verse. Two of these were published and one manuscript was lost.*

CHICKEN

I know enough not to count
my chickens before they hatch.
But what about afterwards?

The old chicken yard greets me
at the end of my uphill climb.
Or, the archeological remains of it,
I should say.
I see it standing as if it were yesterday.
I understand that phrase now.
How phantoms of a person's past
loom up more real than what clearly is not there.

This chicken yard, then, now leveled
and grown over with Johnson grass,
the most stubborn weed in the world.
I can still step inside
the foundation of the first coop
where Great Aunt Mim leaned too far
to collect eggs from a hanging basket.
The stool kicked out from under her.
Her shoulder broke, like hen's eggs.
Later, she claimed, "But, I was being careful."

In the kitchen yesterday my niece
nervously watched me stand on a chair
and strain to reach the top shelf
to put away a cookie canister.
"Wouldn't you rather use the step stool?"
The tactful voice of caution.
No, but, don't worry. I'm being careful.

We both laughed, in joint homage
to a family story footnote.

My friends in subdivisions
lived in split level houses,
but didn't have a split level hen house to play in.

Nor did they have a clutch of stories to hatch.
No ancestors, who, never chicken,
played chicken with the odds.

Aged chicken manure fertilized
Mother's flowers gardens.
Day lilies grew out of it.
Somewhere chickens watched
and ran as if their heads
had just been cut off.

GATED COMMUNITY

Three gates protected our hilltop kingdom.
One at the bottom,
just past the No Trespassing sign.
One at the top,
just short of our house.
And, the gate that barred the back way,
our winter escape route.

If you belonged to the place,
then you possessed keys to the kingdom.
Invaders lived to regret it.

Sometimes, the lower gate remained open.
Joy riders got a jolt
when they zipped up the road,
ready to explore
and found the upper gate locked.
It's a long way down when you're backing up.

As for the back gate,
adventure-seekers, who couldn't fling it open,
saw it as some kind of affront to human freedom.

Lovers liked to park in a shaded nook
just off the gravel road
six-inches away from our back gate.
My introduction to sex
was a naked couple dashing out of the woods,
startled.

Some folks brazenly trekked in.
One bunch of scoundrels topped a good evergreen
just to take home an ill-begotten Christmas trophy.

A troupe of teenagers crouched below the pine row.
Tucked their tails and ran when their jig was up.
Their abandoned cache of imported booze
introduced me to alcoholic spirits.
My parents lined up six bottles
in back of their closet
right behind shoes collecting dust bunnies.
Why my tea-totaling parents
didn't pour it down the drain
is still beyond me.

This dark bar stored my secret treasure.
I developed a taste for Grand Marnier,
doled out one thimble at a time,
nervously watching the level go down.

Thieves slipped through
our security system one night,
set to siphon gas from our 300-gallon tank
supplied by the Farm Bureau.
My mother sensed them first.
Sat bolt upright on the back sleeping porch.
"Erwin, wake up!"
My father slipped down to their car.
Calmly pulled the keys out of the ignition.
A neighbor arrived with an unneeded gun.
Pop scored a flash photo
of our gas hose in their gas tank,
license number prominent in the composition.

Road blocked on both ends by other neighbors.
The gas gang stood stock-still,
quaking until the sheriff arrived.
Caught red-handed, they went straight to jail.
Do not pass Go.

Gates swing in
and then swing out.
I hightailed it to foreign parts:
Europe, Africa, Asia, and the Wild West.
But, I still carry
keys to the kingdom.

BUS RUN

My drumbeat feet
round the corner of our private road
that rushes down towards the river.

A bulldozer a decade past
shaved off the sharp bend in the road
to reduce the odds that downhill cars
crashed into uphill cars.

We trudged up this hill
coming home from school.
But, in the morning,
almost always late,
we dashed cross-county across the horse pasture,
panting, to catch the bus.

My shortcut sprint,
carefully clocked at twelve minutes,
etched a path easy to follow.
My book satchel flew from one wing
and my violin case from the other.

Sometimes the bus did stop on its way back
from its upriver route.
I stood on the river's side of the highway,
hoping the driver had a good breakfast that day.

A route is routine after awhile.
Breaking a habit is harder than breaking a horse.

HORSE HEAVEN

Today snow covers
the field that grazed our horses.

If there's a horse heaven then
Tony and Mary
and Santas and Socks and Copper
have all gone to their reward now.

Well, maybe not Mary.
A small, cute pony
that seemed just my size.
But she bucked me off
right after we brought her home.
Right down there at the mailboxes,
darn her hide.
Before we even got her in the barn.
Hurt, too.

Well, maybe not the one whose name
we don't speak anymore, either.
Kicked Pop, tried to send Pop to heaven.
Doctor took out a foot of intestines.
Pop lived.
But even better, the operation solved
the gut-twisters he'd had since the war.

Gary broke Socks
and won barrel-racing trophies.

Amelia wants one.
But the fences are gone now.
The barn is falling down.

Horses.
Humph.

Still, nothing like a canter
across the alfalfa field
on a fine fall day.
It's own kind of heaven.

We set out for our trip home.

FIVE-HORSE HITCH

We flick the lines to reign in time's runaway horse.
The horse neighs and its flanks quiver.
It's a five-horse hitch that pulls this one-person buggy,
in harness for the last time.
Uneven, to be sure, but they were all stabled
in the same barn when we set out on our trip home:
Past, past perfect, present, future, future perfect.

It's not the passenger that weighs so much.
It's the baggage.

GULLY

I raise my head from the ground
where my eyes were glued
to avoid tripping over my feet.

A cleft joins the two curves of the hill,
a dimple that marks its face like Cary Grant's.

Matted grass cushions my steps
pattering over yesterday's mud.

I ran down the hill on this path
to my aunt's house,
to catch the bus,
or to wrangle a horse to ride.

It wasn't cut so deep then.
This cleft seems more like a gully in the making.
In a hundred years, perhaps a ravine.

My upward gaze catches a doe crossing the gully.
She gamely hitches an injured back leg
behind the other three.
A lame deer, running.

LOVING LIBERTY
For Charlie and his dog Liberty, who died March 26, 2005.

Her loves her,
Liberty.
He really loves her.
She's old,
Liberty.
Really old.
But something
went wrong with
Liberty's back right leg.
To save the hind leg,
they had to cut off
two toes.
This old dog Liberty
had to learn new tricks.

Now she limps,
Liberty,
mostly around the house
arranged carefully
just for her…
by the man who loves her.

Loves Liberty
more than anything.
Even though she limps
on her last legs.

WHAT DO THEY KNOW?

What do they know
>of putting up hay
>>seeds mixed with sweat itching inside your shirt?

What do they know
>of digging manure from your stable
>>to plow into broken ground in a big football field garden?

What do they know
>of poking seed into the thawed ground
>>your little fingers rubbed down?

What do they know
>of canning 200 half-gallon tomatoes
>>as steam from the peck-cocks mix with summer sweat?

What do they know
>of being at the mercy of tyrant cucumbers
>>that just won't stop growing?

What do they know
>of being so sick of pickling everything
>>under the sun that there's nothing to do
>>except pull up the vines by moonlight?

What do they know
>of picking cherries perched out of a limb
>>until a body's head grows dizzy?

What do they know
>of staying up until midnight to get
>>a freezer full of strawberries under cover
>>until fingers look like blood?

Spare me sonnets to the wonders of gardening,
as you pull a random weed or two
and think you've really gone back to the land.

MISSOURI AUCTION

The Vincents, Ponticellos, and Maxies
quit their farms. That time is gone now.
Three generations of living lie in quiet piles.

Jostling and bidding we take
hand polished memories
back to Bland, Belle, Bay, Rosebud.

1. Ironstone soap dishes
2. Two love seats, refinished and upholstered
3. Walnut carved wall clocks, extra fine
4. Flying Perfection Empress, the Grand Champion

"Fifty cents, fifty cents, fifty cents—Who'd give a quarter?
Come on, now, we're selling them choice."

"You know what
I'm going to do with that?"
Nobody cared to ask.

Over the rubble of an afternoon
they move on.
Not knowing where to stop.

First published in *Sou'wester*.

These pines are our mothers, aunts, and sisters.

UP UNDER THE PINE ROWS

When I was little and ran away from home,
I ran under the pine rows up on the ridge.
Those Evergreen Heights of ours.
They all have white pine disease now.
It breaks my heart. The dead branches.

"That's the tree I sang on as a boy," Pop says,
on our stroll that has become an inspection walk.
The branch is a beauty,
a low curving upward horse of a branch.

Great Grandpa E. A. Riehl planted these pines.
Grandma Annie named her poems after them.
"On the Heights."

God's heights were the heights she came to know here,
seated underneath these evergreens
on the ridge overlooking the Mississippi.

She carried them
to the Korean Mission Field—and back.
Julia carried them to Europe to Russia to Africa
to Ellsworth Avenue in Pittsburgh—and back.
I carried them to Ghana to Botswana to Europe to Bhutan
to New Mexico to Northern California—and back.
Gary carries them 60 miles north to his lake
above Jacksonville—and back—and back—and back.

And so, when I was little and ran away from home,
with some food stuffed in my pockets,
quite naturally,
I ran under the pine rows up on the ridge.
Those Evergreen Heights of ours.
(Each time I swore it would be forever,
but my forevers never lasted more than an hour.)
I flung myself under that pony branch,
prayed it would rear its way over me as it
stampeded towards me. Flung myself face down
for my cry. Then faced upward towards the sky.

These pines are our mothers and aunts and sisters.
They are the resting place for ashes at the end.
And now, they too, are dying.

Grandpa Riehl with chestnut variety he grafted.

WALKING RIEHL LANE

At last! Out the door of the Big Brown House
(#1 Thompson Drive)
with my bird's head cane.
Cumulus clouds diffuse the sun's rays
and shoot into the Mississippi River
like God's fingers.

Past the white and brown cottages
that housed summer boarders in the olden days.
"Our best crop," said Grandpa Riehl.
It's a ways up the road to the ridge of pine rows.
Our Evergreen Heights.

On my right rises the old hay field.
Now grass stubble rolls towards the woods.
No hay to harvest.
No sickle pears, either.
Pears just large enough
to fill the palm of your hand.
Their leathery skins yielded to sweet flesh
and juice gushed down my chin.
No pear honey to put up
in the root cellar this year.

At our boundary line
I nip around the white metal gate
and "No trespassing" sign.
"Posted. Erwin Thompson.
Member of the Farm Bureau."
The lane leads on, below overhanging trees.
It's not ours, but it's ours to keep up.
This winter Gary cut through a maze of logs.
There's the ravine filled with old washers,
red bricks, and rusted Maxwell House Coffee cans.
Some things don't change.

Two dogs bark without bites at the Old Lorenz Place.
I meet their master at the plow blade mailbox.
Then Trixie and Misty.
"Riehl? As in Riehl Lane?"
E-yah.
"Mighty sorry to hear about your sister."

To me, it will always be the Old Lorenz Place.
To my father, it's the Old Forees Place.
This caretaker dreams of surfin'

and lets the house run downhill.
Soybean and cornfields farmed out.

Round the corner there's the transformer shed.
Poison ivy, brown and red,
creeps up its locked door with its open hasp.

Gravel, then black top.
Wind sweeps the open plain.
The Old Maupin Place pops up just ahead.
As a girl I walked the mile here to fetch mail.
It's just not right that there's no house set back on the lawn.
Ancient oak towering overhead.
Halfway now.

Blossom Lane crosses Riehl Lane at the 14343 block.
New fangled name.
New fangled county surveyor numbers.
A new era born in brick houses built all in a row.
A painted pallet propped against the hill bears
nine red and white stripes and
twenty-one stars on the field of blue.
Blind patriotism trumps history.

An engine growls behind and I run off the road.
An SUV whizzes by and honks.
Grandma Elliott's cottage at the bottom of the Maupin hill.
We took tea with her.

A hundred yards further the Pivodas lived.
A principal with red hair and red skin fathered
four freckled daughters, playmates of ours.
One day I'm lucky enough to meet Connie,
and finally have a friend here.

I count my steps now; swing my cane.
1-2-3-4 shut the door.
5-6-7-8 close the gate.
There's a rhythm again.

Cut earth ripples beyond the culvert head.
A grader cleared the ditch edged with dead leaves.
Time flashes past quickly along the next stretch.
The bustling factory behind the Elliott house.
Alan and wife moved.
No one lives in the house.
Trucks filled with lumber and pipe
turn into the receiving entrance.
I stand stock still, taking stock.

Charlie Freeman lived right there.
He died in February.
His wife died six months later.
He and Pop integrated the Cub Scout troop.
No rumor would oust his son's right to belong.
"We Freemans have lived here for over 100 years.
We never had any trouble.
Must be these new people causing the trouble."
Table by table he went.
"Does anybody here object? No?
Here? Here? Well, then Jimmie's in."
I met Jimmie, at 57, raking leaves on the family lawn
weeks after his mom passed away.
We sat on the tailgate of his pick-up
and couldn't shut-up about old times.

The Stiritz place torn down.
All green field. The Elliott's bought it.
Yet a phantom tar shack is still there for me

where little Norma lived, smart as a whip, but poor.
She's a looker now and lives in Arizona.

Alvin Middlecoff lives right at the end of the lane.
He cried with me one day,
just after he had to put his mom in the nursing home.
She ran away from him one too many times.
He couldn't keep her safe.

Where the lane meets the hard road,
there's the sign: Riehl Lane and Grafton Road.
Two rivets hold it. The wind whooshes by,
Whistling Dixie

Lakeside

PHONE CALL

It's a relief to be in my West Coast Home.
Talking long distance to my Midwest Home.
Saying, *Good morning, how did your night go?*
Rather than being part of that day and night.

"Ruth, get on the phone!
It's your youngest daughter.
Your daughter, Ruth."

It's me, Mom. Janet.
Your youngest daughter.
"So it was announced."
I crack up.
"Such a pleasure to hear your voice.
Such a nice surprise."
Mom says over and over,
A loop that's easy on the ears.

I got home safely.
"I'm glad," Pop says.
"But, I'm sure no one is more glad than you are."

There was air turbulence on the last leg home.
But it worked out okay.

"Can't control the air."
Nope.

CLARIFYING QUESTIONS (AND ONE ANSWER)

"We'll have to call you back."
That means something's not going well.
Because I've been there, I can picture it all too clearly.

What's my role in this?
How close do I want to be when my parents die?
Can I just roll with the punches?
The clarifying question used to be:
What effect does this have on my health?
This question remains.
But my grief cake layers my growth cake.

Which node is my growth on this tree of life?
Am I a branch that will sway,
not break off from the family trunk?
Can I rise up swinging through life's seasons?
Fertilize and prune as my parents did for me?

("It's the bending and swaying that strengthens the roots,"
a friend tells me. "When a tree is staked from two sides,
it makes the trunk grow straight."
Our bonds are the roots.
Our roots are our foundation,
Where we come from.)

Can I be blessed into usefulness?
Have no regrets?

Back and forth

SHUTTLE SERVICE

"Which place is better?" Mother, on the phone.
I don't know, Mom. That's what I'm trying to find out.

My malady, if that's what it is,
reverses the grass is always greener.
The fence is too high to see one world from the next.

Each place, a world of its own.
Sealed off, except for phone.
In one world,
the other disappears into the world of lost socks.
A magic trick, of sorts.

Back and forth and around she goes.
Where she stops, nobody knows.

It's a relief to be back home.

HOME SWEET HOME

It's a relief to be home in Lake County.
Where Mount Konocti replaces limestone cliffs.
Clear Lake rather than the muddy Mississippi.
Views from our windows stretch miles.

Friends serve as family.
People to visit that I'm not related to.
No one to dress but myself.

A chance to get my hair cut.
My back
back in whack.
My energy channels
needled.

My med mix
officially stamped.

"How sweet it is to be loved by you.
It's like sugar sometimes."

Back in the land of fresh focaccia
and mufaletta mix.
Young mozzarella and basil.

Back in the land of manzanita
and oak bearing mistletoe.
Some trunks have fallen
across the path since my last visit.

There's the Great Blue!
He tests his toes on the Monet bridge
before playing You Can't Catch Me
as I walk along the canal.

A red-shouldered hawk
heads for a Valley Oak, frog in his claws.
The water level seems lower than usual.
The ranger shows me the rain graph when I ask.
But, there's always March.

Yes, it's a relief to be back home.

QUAIL VISITATION

Daniel cleaned twin windows facing the mountain.
Cleared away grime two years in the making.
I cooked supper while he looked out.
"What a shame when birds slam into glass."
Then, suddenly, one did.
A big sound. Then, down.
Tiger prowled the deck to claim his surprise supper.
Then jumped up on the screen to announce the meal.

We scrambled outside.
The oval body, more than stunned.
Dead. Neck broken on glass masquerading as air.
Quail.
We'd never seen one fly so high.
Never seen one so close.
Never held one in my hands.
Hunters must all the time.
Topknot dangling. Eyes closed. Heart stopped.
So many shades, soft gray and brown scalloped with black.
Still feet and pointed toes.

"Do you want me to bury it?"
No, I'll lay it at the top of the land.
At the edge of the woods
where the mountain lion roam at night.
Sing a prayer for its soul
to soar higher than houses with solid air.
To soar into another life quicker than coveys
scurry through dry grasses in the moonlight.

The cat—pacing, pacing the deck.
Excited by its whiff of wildness.
I led him outside, in the opposite direction.
If he hunts for it, all right.
But the quail deserves a head start.

BODY BUDDY

Last night I cuddled around my sweetheart's slim frame,
made more slender by my absence.
The boy doesn't know how to eat unless someone feeds him.

I dreamed his body was my mother's body.
The body I now know better than my own.
The pendulous breasts of old age,
earned in part by suckling three children.

We were born out of this body,
a fact that's more clear to me
now that I've tended her body
as a cross of nurse, lover, and daughter.

Her body is the body of my future.
Already, I'm on the downhill slope towards my death,
assuming I limp through old age to find it.

My breasts can no longer be called
perky in a miracle of defying gravity.
Now they comply with gravity,
and start their descent to my ribcage.
Mother and I weigh the same.
Our bellies begin to look the same.
Mine slightly more toned.
She is the best looking 89-year-old woman we know.

Back home, though,
I no longer have to think
about anyone else's shit but my own.

FOURTH "R"

My "R's" are dwindling.
Fading.
Dissolving into nothingness,
like an eroded clay wall.

And, I, too, am dwindling.
Fading.
Dissolving into nothingness
like an old clay wall
after many storms.

CIRCLING AROUND HOLES

There are the holes in our heads.
Holes in our hearts.
Holes in our lives.
Caves sealed too long
and suddenly unsealed, spew out
centuries of old air. Ah, clean emptiness.

Woodpeckers drill holes in oak trees.
Squirrels scurry right behind packing them
with acorns for a winter feast.

Wind, rain and time
carve caves out of rocky hillsides
where bears go to sleep it off.
There are so many hidey-holes.
Cozy places we wait it out.
Safe places that become dangerous
if we stay too long and lose our sense and sanity.

Down the street at the donut shop,
bakers sell holes by the dozen.
Empty space in the middle of the donut.
Plump flesh, round and ready to roll.
Holes made fresh daily.

ASHES WASHED CLEAN
for Teresa Ebel and Andria and Thomas

Still in a tin can wrapped in gift paper,
her ashes settled, collecting no dust.
The ribbon and paper slipped off easily.
We opened the lid to see the labeled plastic bag,
split at the bottom, ashes sifting onto the newspaper
shielding the kitchen table.

"Do you want a spoon?"
I spooned a tiny bit of that which had been her
into white envelopes lodged inside
a black lacquer box.
The tin, re-wrapped, went back
to its place on the mantle.
The traveling ashes rode with us
along the Northern California Coast.

With us, they saw the sea lions on the rocks
at dusk off Point Arena Lighthouse.
With us, they witnessed the rainbow
that danced on forever,
now close at hand, now far away.
"Do you think we could find
the pot of gold this time?"
"Look! It's right there!"
And it was, until we got there.
Luminous and vibrant. Both there and not there.

The next morning the waves were high,
whipped by the wind. We fed the sea spirits
strawberry frosted-cake and apples,

found our own tide pool
where we gathered clam shells.
Scrambling up rocks,
holding onto each other,
lest we slip into the sea,
we cast in the clam shells a memory at a time.

We fingered her silky ashes,
surprised by bone fragments.
Then, each offered
a pinch of ashes to the frothing sea,
like salt into rising bread dough.

On a coast their mother loved,
we gave her ashes to the sea.
Our first time there and her last.
Like the rainbow,
she was both there and not there.
In life she had traveled through rugged waters.
But, now she had gone beyond,
leaving memories, ashes, and a love
washed clean
in waves thundering offshore.

First appeared in *Palo Alto Review*, Spring 2002, vol. XI, no. 1 as an essay.

The quiet is deep with all the summer people gone.

FALL AT THE LAKE

It is fall at the lake now, no question.
The water cold and roughened by the wind.
The ducks have flown through.
To keep the falling oak leaves
and redwood needles at bay,
I sweep my wooden porch at least once a day.
We had our first rain last night,
sustained and gentle
as it fell on the roof and slid off.

No longer able to swim because of the cold,
I've started walking in the nearby state park.

Each day, something new.

Today, a covey of quail on top of a brush pile.
A dozen wild turkeys foraged in the rain-damp
earth at a deserted camp site. Deer came down
from the hills and peeked onto the path,
holding me in their wide-eyed gaze.
Two turtles sunned on a log.
Then, one slid down,
as if on a children's playground.
When I looked under the log in that world
of dark shadows and reflected branches,
I saw a red crayfish dart.

The quiet is deep
with all the summer people gone.
There is a feeling of sadness
attuned to the darkening
of the shorter days
and longer nights.

STAY A LITTLE LONGER

Yesterday, a friend called.
"He shot himself. He left notes.
I don't know how my daughter will take it.
Listen, and let me know, okay?"

An hour later, I heard her go into mourning.
One might say "hysterics,"
but what I heard was the cry of grief.
That sound took me back
to a ritualized mourning I witnessed
in northwestern Ghana decades ago.

Guardian relatives
led the widow by a rope tied around her waist
while she keened her good-bye song.
The rope, a lifeline,
connected her to life and sanity.
It kept her on this side for her allotted time.
The rope reminded her to resist
the temptation to slip over
to the other side in search of her husband's spirit.

As the daughter next door voiced her pain,
I thought of my connection
to the man who died by his own hand.
He is a man I never knew or met.
I only know him
through hearing stories of how this community was built.
I have walked on steps and pathways he made
from the tail ends of concrete used to pour foundations.
I live in a cabin his hands shaped.

I feel his passing with surprising sharpness.
My thoughts travel to his final day of life.
I wonder at the pain that drove his destruction.

Today, I hear shrieks
on the wide lawn and at the end of the dock
as someone's skin
meets air and water—sounds of children playing.
Laughter drifts
over the water from a party in the works.

The air holds
all these sounds without preference or bias.
Sounds of playing, mourning, and laughing all emerge
from the same throat, heart, and body.

News of other suicides—by hanging—filters in.
I grieve for those who saw the door ajar and left early.
If only all these early-leavers
could have decided
to close that cracked door
between the worlds and stay a little longer.

First appeared in *Palo Alto Review*, Spring 2002, vol. XI, no. 1 as an essay.

The world of our Ancestors

ANNIVERSARY

August 16, 2005

Julia's one year anniversary.

You've been in the world of our ancestors for a year now.

Six years older, you always went before me.

Then, last year, you passed through.

I can't say "passed on."

No. You'll never pass on.

You're too fierce and present for that.

You passed over the waters in the famous boat.

Probably rowed it yourself.

Come on, confess. Didn't you?

Said to the helmsman.

"Sit down, take a rest.
Let me take over for a little while.
You look like you haven't slept in a million years."
And, while you were at it, redesigned the boat
for greater comfort and speed.
Sewed some new boat cushions on the way over,
in-between oar-strokes.
Then, docked, stepped out on that far shore.
Claimed it as your own.

A year. How can that be?
I woke up a year ago:
Not knowing
my life was about to be changed forever.
Not knowing
this date would be carved in flesh and blood.
How innocent I was that morning.
That morning when I woke up,
not knowing.

My brother called.
I heard it in his voice.
Death. Or, at least something terribly off.
Only, I thought it was Mom or Dad.

My dear, sainted, brother.
To have to make that call.
A call no one should ever have to make.
Julia, you would have spit it all out on the spot.
But, Gary, he just didn't want to tell me.
"There's some good news and some bad news."
Well, let's hear the bad news first.
But, he couldn't.
They'd been to the state fair in Springfield.

The hog judging contest.
Seen two college friends, now farmers.
Boys I'd dated—he'd arranged it, of course.
Anything for his little sister.

Please, Gary, I can hear it in your voice.
Please. I'm dying here.
And, so, finally, Julia-like, he spit it out.
"There was a car accident. Julia was killed."
A silence between us, beyond stunned.
Ten seconds of dead air time.
She, who was bottled vitality.
No. No. I'm sorry. Just flat-out, No.

And so our year as a newly-configured family began.
She who loved puzzles, created one.
A family made with a shape cut out.
A family solving a puzzle with a puzzle-piece missing.
A family formed by a void around a dominant figure.
You can't fill the hole.
Even graves don't do that.
And, you cannot airbrush the ghost out of the family picture.

A year of markers:
Her memorial, people spilling out onto the sidewalk.
Thanksgiving and Christmas.
New Years.
Valentine's Day.
March 13th, Julia's birthday.
The court case, finally appearing and closed.
(The law can be so whimsical.)
Someplace in there, the estate finally settled.

Then, there are the markers of the heart.
From the No! and curses
to tenderness and tears.
The Bay of Rage and Vally of Fears.
Endless terrains to transverse.

Four-year-old Maggie led the way.
"Sometimes, I feel Grammy Julia's heart in my heart."
Grammy Julia is dead, she knows that.
But Grammy Julia still loves her.
She knows that, too.

Here at Clear Lake, we commemorated Julia's anniversary.
They do that in Ghana.
They do that in Spain.
They do that in Tibet.
We did that here, this year.
A week of remembrance.
A week of acquired sisterhood.
Remembering to remember to remember.
Re-membering when the member is severered.
Remembering the water of life.

Four mothers and two sisters
lost among us this past twelve-month.
We honored them in ceremony at the sulfur caves.
The eagle of the North keeping the vision.
The mouse of the South
scurrying close to the ground, carrying the details.
Beginnings in the East.
Endings and apparent endings in the West.
Washing our hands from the calabash.

Watering Meg's shrine among the oak roots.
The moss springing instantly from brown to green.

Annelle fixed my cobra squirt gun
(years of Mommy-training, she said)
so that plastic striped snake could wash away our
words spoken that became venom.
We doused for water with my clay rods.
They never fail when used beside a body of water.
The Water of Life is all around us and inside us, after all.

My clay sceptor passed from hand to hand as the talking stick.
Stories spoken around the Water Banner
we swayed with in the stream.
Then, food, pictures, and poems on the lawn.
Gifts from the gift blanket.
Good-bye for now.

(A month later, Melissa called in the directions
once more and asks Grandmother to bless us
on the same creek shores.
The water that much lower.
The ceremony officially closed.)

Today, supporting from her home,
Lucy lights candles and incense
when she cleans her Japanese family altar, the Butsudan,
a ritual she chooses to do today
"to acknowledge and honor that there truly is no pain,
nor absence of pain;
that all is life and it continues and transforms."
Let's hear it for the Heart Sutra!

Last year and this, my electronic *Glimpse of the Day* tells me:
"Bereavement can force you to look at your life directly,
compelling you to find a purpose in it
where there may not have been one before.
When suddenly you find yourself alone
after the death of someone you love,
it can feel as if you are being given a new life
and are being asked:
What will you do with this life?
And why do you wish to continue living?
Pray for help and strength and grace.
Pray that you will survive and discover
the richest possible meaning
to the new life you now find yourself in.
Be vulnerable and receptive.
Be courageous and patient.
Above all, look into your life
to find ways of sharing your love
more deeply with others now."

There are many layers of grief,
and each of us grieves in our own way.
Bereft—shorn, torn open, last year.
Three gigantic earth-moving machines
on the property next door.

They growled and grumbled all day long
as they dug further and further into the side of the hill,
leaving a mountain of earth in their wake.
I felt they were digging a gigantic grave for Julia.
But no grave could ever hold her.

And, now, this year?
The house is for sale.

The joke?
It's butt ugly.

So, be careful of the house you build.
Julia's house needed painting,
but was structurally sound.
As her husband Dave said,
"Hers was a gallant, hopeful, helpful,
effective life. The ripples from it reach
astonishing numbers of people.
It seems reasonable to hope
that the ripples will continue onward
through generations
and circumstances
at which we can only guess.
But surely some of that is visible among you now."

I still find myself alone
after the death of someone I love,
I still feel as if I have been given a new life
and am being asked:
What will I do with this life?
And why do I wish to continue living?
What of the house that I will build,
now that the earth has been moved?

My journey and my family's journey
of bereavement continues
as the moon waxes towards fullness.
Thank heavens the stars are up there in the sky,
"all secret and wise twinkling down," as Melissa says,
as we, breathing,
look up at the moon.

About the Author

Janet Grace Riehl is an award-winning author, artist, performer, and creativity coach. Her poems, stories, and essays have been widely published in national literary magazines such as *Harvard Review* and the newly-released anthology *Stories to Live By: Wisdom to Help You Make the Most of Every Day*. Her life moves between two great bodies of water—the Mississippi River in Southwestern Illinois and Clear Lake in Northern California.

978-0-595-37499-1
0-595-37499-9

Printed in the United States
44303LVS00006B/244-264